The D.N.A. of Communion
75-Day Devotional

Understanding Your God-Given Divine & Natural Authority

S. Sylvi Anderson

Emery Press LLC
Fort Lauderdale, FL
www.emerypressbooks.com

All rights reserved.

First Edition – November 2021

Copyright 2021 – S. Sylvi Anderson

No part of this book may be reproduced or transmitted in any form or by any means, electronic or mechanical, including photocopying, recording, or by any information storage or retrieval system, permitted by law. For additional information, contact Emery Press Books.

Permissions:
Partial lyrics from "Freedom" by Matthew Bushard, licensed by CapitolCMG.
Image of DNA Strand © Sergey Khakimullin from Dreamstime.com.
Scriptures:
- The Expanded Bible. Copyright 2011 by Thomas Nelson.
- The Holy Bible, New International Version®, NIV® Copyright 1973, 1978, 1984, 2011 by Biblica, Inc.®
- The Amplified Bible, Classic Edition (AMPC). Copyright 1954, 1958, 1962, 1964, 1965, 1987 by The Lockman Foundation.
- The Living Bible. Copyright 1971 by Tyndale House Foundation.
- The Passion Translation®. Copyright 2017, 2018, 2020 by Passion & Fire Ministries, Inc.

ISBN (softcover): 978-0-9600505-8-1
ISBN (ebook): 978-0-9600505-9-8

Edited by Russ Womack
Additional Edits by Leila Anderson
Interior Design by Wendy C Garfinkle
Cover Design by Sweet 15 Designs

Contents

Foreword 13
About Communion 17
Author's Note 19
Introduction 21
Day 1 22
    The Bread: Consecration 22
    The Cup: Covenant 23
Day 2 24
    The Bread: Righteousness 24
    The Cup: Holiness 25
Day 3 26
    The Bread: The Heart of It 26
    The Cup: Seals the Commitment 27
Day 4 28
    The Bread: Resting in Jesus 28
    The Cup: Boldness 29
Day 5 30
    The Bread: Gratitude 30
    The Cup: Praise 31
Day 6 32
    The Bread: Restoring Peace 32
    The Cup: Refreshing 33
Day 7 34
    The Bread: Relationship 34
    The Cup: D.N.A. (Divine and Natural Authority) 35
Day 8 36
    The Bread: Forgiveness 36
    The Cup: Salve 37
Day 9 38
    The Bread: Divine Compass! 38
    The Cup: Salvation 39
Day 10 40

The Bread: Devotion **40**
The Cup: Focus **41**
Day 11 42
   The Bread: Tangible **42**
   The Cup: Connection **43**
Day 12 44
   The Bread: The Word of God **44**
   The Cup: Revelation **45**
Day 13 46
   The Bread: Flesh/Body Submission **46**
   The Cup: Cleansing **47**
Day 14 48
   The Bread: Discipline **48**
   The Cup: Forgiveness **49**
Day 15 52
   The Bread: Repentance **52**
   The Cup: Power **53**
Day 16 54
   The Bread: Brazen **54**
   The Cup: Renewal **55**
Day 17 56
   The Bread: Anointing **56**
   The Cup: Newness of Life **57**
Day 18 58
   The Bread: No Condemnation **58**
   The Cup: Unrecognized Power **59**
Day 19 60
   The Bread: Connection **60**
   The Cup: Superhighway Flow **61**
Day 20 62
   The Bread: Priorities **62**
   The Cup: Authority **63**
Day 21 66
   The Bread: Your Focus **66**
   The Cup: Family **67**

Day 22 .... **68**
    The Bread: Makes a Way **68**
    The Cup: The Blood is for the Redeemed **69**
Day 23 .... **70**
    The Bread: Path **70**
    The Cup: Protection **72**
Day 24 .... **74**
    The Bread: Understanding **74**
    The Cup: Marks You **75**
Day 25 76
    The Bread: Willing **76**
    The Cup: Are You the One? **78**
Day 26 80
    The Bread: Unhinged **80**
    The Cup: You Are the Access Point **81**
Day 27 84
    The Bread: Boldness in Confidence **84**
    The Cup: Refreshing **85**
Day 28 86
    The Bread: Do Not Mourn **86**
    The Cup: Priceless Pearls **87**
Day 29 90
    The Bread: Roots Out What is Destroying You! **90**
    The Cup: The Blood of Jesus Peels Back the Layers **91**
Day 30 94
    The Bread: Making Bread **94**
    The Cup: All of You **96**
Day 31 98
    The Bread: Silence **98**
    The Cup: Covers Your Sins **99**
Day 32 100
    The Bread: Embrace God's Revelation of the Next Layer of the Onion **100**
    The Cup: Healing Salve **102**
Day 33 104

The Bread: Purposeful	104
The Cup: Blood is a Multi-Faceted Diamond	106
Day 34	108
The Bread: He Did It For All!	108
The Cup: Power Wash	109
Day 35	110
The Bread: No Other Way!	110
The Cup: Ever-Flowing River	111
Day 36	112
The Bread: Missing the Invitation Call!	112
The Cup: The Last Gift	114
Day 37	116
The Bread: Help to Forgive	116
The Cup: Blood Replacement	118
Day 38	120
The Bread: Not Always Perfect	120
The Cup: Easy to Neglect	121
Day 39	124
The Bread: Determined Focus	124
The Cup: Bloodshed Must Occur	126
Day 40	128
The Bread: Bodies on the Ground	128
The Cup: Written In Blood	130
Day 41	132
The Bread: Humanness	132
The Cup: Enjoying the Time	134
Day 42	136
The Bread: Last Meal	136
The Cup: Share	137
Day 43	138
The Bread: Chose to Die!	138
The Cup: Jesus Died to His Humanness so Your Humanity Would Not Be the Death of You	139
Day 44	142
The Bread: Living Sacrifice	142

The Cup: New Covenant 143
Day 45 144
　The Bread: No More Shackles, No More Chains! 144
　The Cup: Determination 146
Day 46 148
　The Bread: Once Bitten, Twice Shy! Stretch! 148
　The Cup: Many Will Not Believe! 149
Day 47 152
　The Bread: Old Ways 152
　The Cup: Conscious Effort 154
Day 48 156
　The Bread: Sustenance 156
　The Cup: Wound Care! 158
Day 49 160
　The Bread: Take Up Your Cross! 160
　The Cup: Time to Drink! 162
Day 50 164
　The Bread: Die To Self 164
　The Cup: It Is Available To You! 165
Day 51 166
　The Bread: Turn Back To Jesus! 166
　The Cup: Get Refilled! 168
Day 52 170
　The Bread: Daily Bread! 170
　The Cup: Never Thirst Again! 172
Day 53 174
　The Bread: Full Meal Deal 174
　The Cup: Your Blood Does Not Lie! 175
Day 54 176
　The Bread: True Love 176
　The Cup: The Color Red! 177
Day 55 178
　The Bread: God's Grace 178
　The Cup: Mercy 179
Day 56 180

The Bread: Deliverance from Enemies!	180
The Cup: Justified	181
Day 57	182
The Bread: Deliverance from Affliction	182
The Cup: The Blood	183
Day 58	184
The Bread: Deliverance From Adversity	184
The Cup: My Blood Does Not Skip Generations!	185
Day 59	188
The Bread: Enablement!	188
The Cup: Comforter and Guide!	189
Day 60	190
The Bread: Daily Guidance	190
The Cup: Your History	191
Day 61	192
The Bread: Forgiveness	192
The Cup: Transfusion Time!	193
Day 62	194
The Bread: Preservation	194
The Cup: Cover You With My Blood!	197
Day 63	198
The Bread: Barabbas	198
The Cup: Cover me!	199
Day 64	202
The Bread: Mental Anguish	202
The Cup: Incubated!	203
Day 65	204
The Bread: Let Jesus Be Your Simon!	204
The Cup: Simon Was The Last	205
Day 66	206
The Bread: Cross To Bear!	206
The Cup: Legacy-Making!	208
Day 67	210
The Bread: Always Ready!	210
The Cup: Blood & Water = Holy Spirit	211

- **Day 68** 212
  - The Bread: Car Care 212
  - The Cup: Let This Cup Pass! 213
- **Day 69** 214
  - The Bread: Transports 214
  - The Cup: Drink It! 215
- **Day 70** 216
  - The Bread: What is Significant! 216
  - The Cup: Being Resolved! 217
- **Day 71** 218
  - The Bread: Maintenance 218
  - The Cup: All Must Drink 219
- **Day 72** 220
  - The Bread: Keeping Healthy! 220
  - The Cup: (D)ivine Health is our Standard 221
- **Day 73** 224
  - The Bread: Washed and Cleaned! 224
  - The Cup: Purity 225
- **Day 74** 226
  - The Bread: Spiritual Washing and Cleaning! 226
  - The Cup: The Flow from the Throne 227
- **Day 75** 228
  - The Bread & The Cup: 228
- **Acknowledgments** 231
- **About the Author** 233

Foreword

ONE OF THE MOST DIFFICULT THINGS FOR A WRITER to do is stand out. To be set apart from the hundreds of thousands of aspiring authors across the globe. Even more tasking is creating something that has been written a thousand times before to sound different, new, eye-catching, thought-provoking. How does one discuss popular historical events and shed new light on them? How does one write with a new twist while keeping the truth intact? The birth of Christ, the baptism of Christ, the 3-year missionary journey of Christ, and the crucifixion of Christ. one runs a risk at re-writing on these subjects – a risk that entails an audience who has already heard the story, and therefore might choose to skim the pages rather than dive into them. The same rings true with the events surrounding The Last Supper that Christ held with His disciples. And along with The Last Supper, the breaking of the bread and drinking of the wine (or grape juice), symbolizing the body and blood of Christ.

Historical events that run years or decades, such as the major wars throughout history, allow the author greater freedom to add, subtract, or embellish on the events, but with such a narrow timeline, something that most likely occurred over a short few hours in one room, the last meal Christ shared with His disciples prior to His arrest and subsequent crucifixion, is set in a confined space and time with no wiggle room to brush different colors upon the facts.

To write about such a holy event recounted across Christian churches around the world each Sunday is admirable by itself. But then to make it relatable, informational, and with a graceful pathway toward a greater and closer relationship with God is remarkable. So, the question remains: how do you recount a well-known, holy event that has been practiced for more than two millennia, and make it fresh, new, and exciting?

Author S. Sylvi Anderson has achieved just that. She has written the masterful 75-day devotional, *The D.N.A. of Communion*, which you hold in your hands.

The D.N.A. of Communion is broken down into two separate readings each day: The Bread and The Cup. Relevant and thought-provoking scriptures headline each day's devotionals, followed by a recitation relating to the scriptures for the reader to learn, research, and ponder. S. Sylvi then masterfully encourages her readers to speak out their own prayer, by giving what she calls a Prayer Starter.

Upon reading her book, I found myself revisiting scriptures I had read before, and reflecting upon new ones that I had never seen but were just as impactful. How the scriptures relate to S. Sylvi's daily commentaries is uncanny and effective, and prompted me to re-read them as they are woven within the sentences in the related passages. The Prayer Starter is also masterful, in that I found myself unconsciously using them as a springboard for my own words – just God and me. My voice softened as the Holy Spirit spoke, guided, counseled, and comforted me.

S. Sylvi doesn't leave out anything with her devotional. Righteousness, gratitude, forgiveness, repentance, anointing, and the mind-blowing topic of D.N.A. (Divine and Natural Authority), among many others. Each of the 140 devotionals are prayerfully constructed, purposefully arranged, and gracefully presented to the reader.

I recommend this book to anyone – no matter their religion, belief, situation, past failures, as well as those who feel they're unworthy, or unlovable. Because within these pages you'll discover our God, who forgives, desires to be with you, misses a close relationship with you, and will continue to pursue you in the hopes that you'll turn around and see Him standing there with open arms. I would encourage anyone who is curious about God, is seeking God, has run from God and wants to return to the Father, or has been a lifelong Christian who wants and thirsts for a deeper relationship with the King of Kings to open this must-read devotional and turn to page one. Step in with an open, repentant heart, and listen for our Father's still, small voice. You'll never be the same.

~ Russell Womack, Editor

About Communion

When taking communion, the elements can be whatever you have available. However, Nabisco Mini Saltines will be required for some devotions regarding the bread, and grape or cranberry juice is best for the cup.

There are no set times that you "have to" do the devotion. The bread and cup can be done simultaneously or one in the morning and one at night. Do what works best for you. God loves when you spend time with Him; remember this is not a ritual; it is a relationship!

Author's Note

Welcome to an incredibly intimate and deep calling unto deep time of learning through seeking God daily to clarify who we are and who He is through taking communion. Over the next 75 days, this process you are about to participate in will require you to seek God daily for more profound meanings and thoughts about the bread and cup for communion. Additionally, you will be introduced to the new concept of D.N.A. (Divine and Natural Authority). Throughout the book, deeper and deeper levels of revelation will increase your understanding of God's view of our DNA.

Commit to a daily time with God where He can speak to you, showing you who you indeed are because of what Jesus did for you. Many concepts may challenge the way you have thought and believed, and that is perfectly fine. Allow God to expound on the topics each day by opening your heart, mind, and soul to allow the Holy Spirit to speak, transform, renew, and bring the revelation that will take you to the next level that God desires for you!

You can email the author at: LivingBeyondtheCross@gmail.com

Interact with the author and other readers at Facebook page: https://www.facebook.com/LivingBeyondtheCross

Introduction

RECOGNIZE JESUS.

Communion is not a habit, a ritual, a goal, or a task to check off; it is a relationship. As you experience this time of worship by taking Holy Communion, you'll find something much, much more profound. Do not be lulled into a ritual that is devoid of meaning. God takes communion extremely serious. It is not a game to Him, not a ritualistic act, but rather a connecting and knitting of your flesh/earthly-natural soul and body with His Divine Spirit so that you can receive the authority through the knowledge He desires to reveal. It is recognizing that God, embodied in the form of man (Jesus), came to commune with you in this natural world and to save you from an eternity without Him!

Communion is a principle, a symbolic recognition of Jesus. It is not critical what elements you use for the bread (body) and drink (blood) because it is more than that. It is the meaning, acknowledgment, focus, and posture of worship, thanksgiving, praise, and honor to Jesus, your Lord, and Savior. Take a moment of silence and exude all the love you have for Jesus and allow Him to love you back and to speak directly to you.

Day 1
The Bread: Consecration
Matthew 26:26; Psalm 42:7

*B*efore starting this (deep calling out to deep) journey into God's Divine revelation and a deeper level of understanding of communion and who you are. Take a moment to consecrate yourself. Ask God to open your spiritual eyes and ears for the Holy Spirit to guide and teach you even more.

> **Matthew 26:26 (NIV)**
>
> [26] While they were eating, Jesus took bread, and when he had given thanks, he broke it and gave it to his disciples, saying, "Take and eat; this is my body."

Prayer of Consecration: Lord Jesus, I take this bread now, purposely declaring I agree that just as Your body was broken, and You died, so too my flesh will be broken off and declared dead! Dead to sin, dead to earthly desires and wants. I take this bread that symbolizes Your body to represent the giving of my body entirely to you. I consecrate my body just as you did with a blessing for how Your sacrifice has brought me to this place, and now with the determination and help from the Holy Spirit, I break my body from this earthly realm and power. I break the powers the enemy has had, in Your name, Jesus. I break any ties to the enemy and his lies. And I give my body to You, Jesus. I eat this bread in remembrance that I will daily partake in the death of my flesh and resurrection of an eternal body.

The Cup: Covenant
Matthew 26:27–28, 36–44

*J*esus took the cup:
1. Spoke a prayer of Thanksgiving
2. Then gave it to His disciples and said:
   a. Drink from it, all of you (this included Judas and Peter)
   b. This is my blood, the blood of my covenant and promise with you
   c. It is poured out for many people so that SINS are FORGIVEN.

Jesus knew this was His purpose and destiny. He was demonstrating to His own unbelieving, doubting, and betraying disciples that He would take the cup (in Matthew 26:36–44, He asked God to take the cup, but Jesus signed it in blood). He thanked God, even knowing what was to come because He knew His blood signed the covenant for the forgiveness of sins. Even the disciples' (unbelieving/doubting/betrayers) sins and the sins of ALL others.

Prayer Starter: Lord, I take this cup in remembrance of the signed covenant that You, Jesus, made. Starting with Your blood signature in the Garden of Gethsemane, and through every drop poured out until Your death on the cross. I pray a prayer of thanksgiving for all that his blood represents and for the forgiveness of sins.

Day 2
The Bread: Righteousness
2 Corinthians 5:21; Romans 5:17

*W*e have right standing with God, not for what we have done but because of Jesus and what He did for us. Take some time to thank Jesus for willingly leaving Heaven to come to Earth, being born a man, and living holy and blameless continuously throughout His time here on Earth. His love for us and desire (to right the wrong done when Adam and Eve sinned) was a driving force to sacrifice Himself for us. He knew He would be falsely accused, beaten, and abused, nailed on the cross, and would die. However, He also knew He would take the keys of death and the grave from Satan and resurrect; all so we will be righteous before the Lord. He did it all for us!

Take this bread in remembrance of the gift He gave you— righteousness! Jesus paid the price for you to be approved, acceptable, and in right relationship with God by His goodness.

Prayer Starter: Thank you, Jesus, for the gift of righteousness You gave me. I will never truly understand the pain and agony You went through for me, just as it is often hard for me to comprehend the gift of righteousness, forgiveness of all my sins, and that it is all a free gift from You. Help me live each day with gratitude for all You have done.

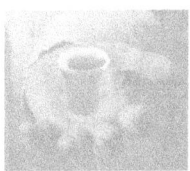

The Cup: Holiness
Leviticus 19:2

Jesus shed his holy blood on Earth — in the courtyard where He was beaten, on the streets as He walked to Calvary, and into the soil under the cross! His holy blood was shed everywhere! Everything Jesus' blood touches becomes holy, including us! When we gave our heart to Jesus, He covered us in His blood; so, when God looks at us, all He sees is the blood of Jesus. When we ask for forgiveness, repent, and renounce all our sins, we can immediately boldly come to our Father God, knowing we are holy before Him.

If you are struggling, ask for help from the Holy Spirit to guide you through renewing your mind, body, and soul. And forgive yourself, knowing Jesus paid the price for your holiness.

Drink from this cup in remembrance of the holiness you have in Christ.

Prayer Starter: Jesus, You shed Your blood so that I can be covered by it. When God looks at me, He sees Your blood, and I am white as snow/pure in His eyes. Thank you for cleansing me from all unrighteousness.

Day 3
The Bread: The Heart of It
2 Thessalonians 2:16–17; James 1:12

It all comes down to a matter of the heart! Jesus' heart longed to please His Heavenly Father. To do God's will, save, redeem, heal, and restore every person. This complete devotion motivated Jesus and provided Him with the power to press on and through every adversity—even the cross! We seek the Lord to give us the strength and power that puts a resolve in our heart, body, soul, and mind to press on through each moment, each adversity, with an unstoppable drive to fulfill God's purpose in and for our life! Jesus demonstrated the highest level of passion and devotion, desiring to see <u>every</u> person know God as He knows God.

Take this bread now to remember what Jesus did at the cross, as well as to commit your heart and life to be His heart and life.

Prayer Starter: Lord, help me persevere through all the trials that may come my way, knowing that You are my source of strength and power. Help me remain strong and resolved just as Your Son Jesus did in all His trials so that I, too, can fulfill Your purpose and plan for my life.

The Cup: Seals the Commitment
Luke 22:41–44

This cup represents the blood of Jesus that sealed the promise of redemption. The blood that began to flow from Jesus even before He emptied Himself at the cross. First, His blood was shed when He died to Himself, sacrificing His will, flesh, fears, and earthly man when He prayed in the Garden of Gethsemane. Jesus sought God, and this was when the first and most critical death occurred. Jesus' blood was shed as He sought God for the resolve, determination, and ability to endure every aspect of all that would ensue. When Jesus was done praying, He was already dead (to the flesh, the carnal man's fears and anxieties) and in the presence of His Lord! Not His will, but the Lord's will was all He saw! He would bear it all for the reward of us being redeemed!

Take this cup to seal your commitment to this next level in the Lord, where you accept that you are redeemed!

Prayer Starter: Lord, for me to go to the next level You want me to go, I too must die to myself, sacrificing my will, my flesh, my fears, my earthly desires. Oh, how difficult this is for me, just as it was for Jesus, and I do not even know what You have in store for me. Jesus shed His blood so that I can call on Your Holy Spirit in me to fill me with the resolve, determination, and ability to endure every aspect of all that You need me to do. I am redeemed from this world's hold that has held me captive to the limits set by it and by the entanglements of my desires. Help me, Lord, to die to self and live for You!

Day 4
The Bread: Resting in Jesus
Matthew 27:51; Hebrews 10:19–22

*J*esus paved the way for us to have communion with our Heavenly Father. By going to the cross, Jesus tore in half the veil that kept us separated from God. We have full access to the throne room! Because of Jesus, we can rest in the Lord's unending love, mercy, and grace. We do not have to work for our acceptance or strive to do enough just so that God will forgive and love us. We can press forward to pursue God's heart and desires for us. We can rest in God because of all Jesus did.

Each day as you take this bread, it is a reminder of the many gifts Jesus gave you. God has forgiven all your sins, your past, your failures, etc., and you are accepted into the presence of the King of kings because you accepted Jesus and made Him Lord of your life!

Prayer Starter: Thank you, Jesus, for dying so that the veil was torn, so I now have full access to God through You! Help me daily to remember that I do not have to work or strive for God's love and acceptance because You provided this costly gift to me as a free gift!

The Cup: Boldness
Galatians 2:20; Luke 9:23

*J*esus' blood provides access to the King of kings, Lord of lords, and the Alpha and Omega. Because of the blood of Jesus, we can walk in boldness to do God's will every moment of every day. That authorizes us to approach the throne of glory, allows us to speak the truth boldly, live pure and holy, and continually grow. Jesus demonstrated the greatest act of boldness by going to the cross, dying, and resurrecting. He died and rose for us to have bold faith in our relationship with God, Him, and the Holy Spirit. Now we must die to self as well—not a physical death, but a death of our flesh, desires, and wants, doing only what God designed us to do.

Take this cup as a commitment to the process of dying to self and living for Christ. Although this is a daily process, you have the Holy Spirit to guide you into complete understanding, and you have Jesus who came to demonstrate it is possible and worth it.

Prayer Starter: Oh Lord, help me understand how to live a life putting my flesh to death so I can live as You desire for me to live. Help my unbelief, help me through the hurdles of letting my will and ways go so that I can do as Jesus did and align my will to Your will for my life. Holy Spirit, bring revelation from the Lord and through the Word of God so that I can walk boldly and have bold faith in God!

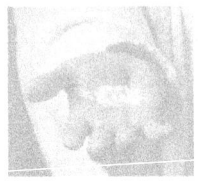

Day 5
The Bread: Gratitude
John 6:48, 51

In John 6:48, Jesus makes it clear that He is the bread of life; in the Expanded Bible, it says, "I am the bread that gives life." Then in John 6:51, Jesus expounds on verse 48, stating, "I am the living bread that came down from Heaven. Whoever eats this bread will live forever. This bread is my flesh, which I will give for the life of the world."

Jesus could not have been any clearer that:
1. He came from Heaven.
2. That the bread represents His flesh—the part that allowed Him to step foot in our plane, Earth.
3. By eating this bread, you will live forever.

The bread represents Jesus, and in this, our gratefulness to take this bread daily in remembrance of Jesus and the sacrifice He was at the cross. But more so, the life He was throughout the Word, and even now throughout every area of our life. Jesus has sustained you in so many ways!

Prayer Starter: Lord, I take this bread in gratitude to Jesus who sacrificed His body, being broken and pierced so that I can have eternal life. Jesus made it possible for me to have constant communication with You, Lord, and to have Your Holy Spirit living within me. I can know that I will always be sustained and made whole because of all Jesus has done!

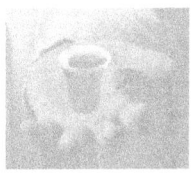

The Cup: Praise
Luke 1:41–44, 4:15; Psalm 150:6; Revelation 5:13

From conception, an angel brought praise as he declared to Mary of Jesus' coming. John the Baptist leaped and praised in His mother's womb when Jesus (also in His mother's womb) came to visit. When Jesus was born, the angels praised, the Magi praised; wherever Jesus went throughout His life, everyone praised! And although His praise was silenced for three days at the cross, no one who believes in Jesus has stopped praising Him since His resurrection. Now, the praise for the blood shed by Jesus for our redemption, healing, restoration, and so much more has forever been and will be permanently on our lips!

Prayer Starter: Lord, I take this cup, representing the blood of Jesus, in remembrance of the praise given to the Lord and Savior Jesus, whom all praise is due. It was by Jesus shedding His blood at Calvary that I can be called Your beloved! As I take this cup, Lord, I do it remembering that my lips shall forever praise Your name.

AFFIRMATIONS

I can rest in God's Love, NOT work for it because of all Jesus did!
Jesus knew His blood signed the covenant for the forgiveness of my sins!
Whatever Jesus' blood touches becomes holy, including me!

Day 6
The Bread: Restoring Peace
Philippians 4:7 Amplified Bible, Classic Edition

Jesus is the restorer of peace — a peace that surpasses all understanding. When Jesus went to the cross, it was in the most chaotic time for everyone. There was no peace anywhere in the world, not in the minds, hearts, or people—nowhere—except in Him! Jesus was at peace because He was doing the will of the Father! He was fulfilling His calling and purpose!

Take this bread as a reminder that when everything seems like chaos all around you, you have within you **ALL** peace—the Godhead[1] lives within you in the Holy Spirit. Jesus demonstrated for you how to be in perfect peace no matter what is going on around you.

Prayer Starter: Thank you, Jesus, for Your perfect peace, a peace that surpasses all understanding. In all the chaos around me, I embrace Your peace God, through Jesus and living within me by Your Holy Spirit.

---

[1] *Godhead = God, Jesus, and the Holy Spirit in one.*

The Cup: Refreshing
Revelation 22:1; Isaiah 33:21; Ezekiel 47:1–12

Jesus' blood is a refreshing flow from the throne. He shed His human blood at the cross and, when resurrected, was filled with God's blood that flows like rivers of life <u>from His throne</u>. When we need refreshing, we have access to the never-ending river of life found in the blood of Jesus. We can call on the blood of Jesus anytime because of what Jesus did at the cross. He tore the veil and broke the boulders in half that blocked us from the river of life!

Drink from this cup in remembrance of the human blood that Jesus shed for eternal blood so you can have access to this mighty rushing river that refreshes, heals, delivers, sets free, restores, renews, and so much more!

Prayer Starter: Oh Lord, I thank You for Your river of life flowing in and through me because of what Your Son, Jesus, did for me.

The blood of Jesus being a refreshing flow from God's throne brought to remembrance the song by Mary A. Lathbury, "Spring Up, O Well, Spring Up:"[2]:

> I've got a river of life flowing out of me
> Makes the lame to walk
> And the blind to see
> Opens prison doors
> Sets the captives free
> I've got a river of life flowing out of me.
> Spring up, O well, within my soul.
> Spring up, O well, and make me whole
> Spring up, O well, and give to me
> That life abundantly.

---

[2] <u>https://hymnary.org/text/spring_up_o_well_spring_up</u>

Day 7
The Bread: Relationship
Ephesians 2:18; Hebrews 10:19–22; John 14:6

Jesus went to the cross and died so we could have an intimate relationship with the Lord. Jesus met every requirement once and for all that allowed us direct access to God—Himself. Without Jesus, this would be impossible. Then Jesus resurrected and ascended back to the Father, who then birthed in us the Holy Spirit who makes us even more like Him—part human, part of/connected to the Godhead.

Take this bread in remembrance of the intimate relationship you have with Christ, your Heavenly Father, and the Holy Spirit.

Prayer Starter: I thank You, Jesus, for providing me direct access to God by sacrificing Yourself on the cross for me! I do not take for granted the gift You have given me. You returned to Heaven so I could forever be connected to You by the comforter, God's Holy Spirit.

The Cup:
D.N.A. (Divine and Natural Authority)
Matthew 28:18–20; Luke 10:19

*J*esus came to, walked, lived, died, and rose on this natural plane. He brought the Divine to Earth and took back the authority from the grips of our enemy, Satan. In Jesus' blood, He carried the D.N.A. (Divine and Natural Authority) that gave Him rulership and dominion on Earth as in Heaven. Jesus shed every drop of His blood at the cross so we could be infused with His blood—His D.N.A. when we accepted Him and were saved. Thus, Jesus' D.N.A. flows in and through us. We have Divine authority and natural authority authorized by the blood of Jesus. Jesus won the battle and took the keys of authority and dominion from Satan. Jesus is the victor!

Take this cup in remembrance of who's D.N.A. flows through your entire being. You look, smell, sound, and are made in the image of Jesus. This alone puts a target on you from Satan but fear not, for Jesus gave you the power to tread on the enemy (Luke 10:19), the authority in His blood that is now infused in you!

Prayer Starter: Lord, help me understand and embrace the Divine and Natural Authority that flows in and through me because of the blood of Jesus and the victory He has given me in my life and this world.

Day 8
The Bread: Forgiveness
Colossians 3:13; Psalm 32:5

Most people know that Jesus went to the cross as the spotless lamb for the FORGIVENESS of our sins. But there is more! Jesus demonstrated to us that even in our own life, true and complete forgiveness is sacrificial. It is not just words, not just a flippant apology, or even worse, an "I'm sorry"! No, true forgiveness requires a resolve to forgive, handing ourselves over to the process of forgiveness, taking the pain of the humiliation and wrath, carrying the burden of forgiveness, then nailing our unforgiveness to the cross of forgiveness. Finally, our flesh, emotions, and thoughts must die to unforgiveness. By having a time for the death of our unforgiveness to come to a resolution while Jesus/Holy Spirit seals the issue and renews our mind, heart, and soul, then comes the best part: we resurrect with absolute true God-given freedom from that bondage. We have resolute forgiveness that forever frees us.

Prayer Starter: Lord, I take this bread asking for Your help through this process. Help me have the resolve to forgive, hand myself over to the process of forgiveness, take the pain of the humiliation and wrath, carry the burden of forgiveness, and then nail my unforgiveness to Your cross of forgiveness. Lord, help me understand and, with Your guidance, go through the process where my flesh, emotions, and thoughts die to the unforgiveness. Thank you in advance for renewing my mind, heart, and soul and for living continually in the absolute, authentic, God-given freedom and forgiveness that only You can give me.

The Cup: Salve
Romans 5:9; Ephesians 1:7; 1 Peter 1:18–19

The blood of Jesus has the divine ability to heal, restore, renew, remove, re-establish, and so much more in every area of our life. The Holy Spirit is working in and through us, bringing to light the places in us that must be rooted out and destroyed at the cross. God did not leave us to have gaping wounds left there— no, He provided us with the blood of Jesus that fills us and is a salve that heals the deep wounds that we have hidden in the recesses of our body, mind, and soul. Only with the collaboration of all three in the Godhead can this process occur. The blood of Jesus is a salve that has healing power that is indescribable and life-changing.

Take this cup in remembrance of the price Jesus paid to provide the healing salve of His blood so you can be healed and restored on Earth as you already are in Heaven!

Drink from this cup now and ask God for the blood of Jesus to begin the healing process in you as you do.

Prayer Starter: Jesus, I need healing, and nothing will heal me like the salve that comes from Your blood. I ask that You heal and restore me with Your healing blood that heals, restores, renews, removes, and re-establishes wholeness in me.

Day 9
The Bread: Divine Compass!
Romans 12:2; 2 Corinthians 5:21; Hebrews 4:15; Matthew 11:25–27

*J*esus sacrificed his humanness and flesh, not just at the cross but every day of His life! He was sinless, yet He walked as we do on this earth for 33 years under harsher conditions than we can imagine. Daily, moment-by-moment, Jesus directed His heart and focus on and to the desires of His Father. Yes, He still had to live and function as we do, yet He demonstrated how to keep our Heavenly Father as our compass. Jesus was sustained and operated by the will of the Father

Each day as you take this bread, be reminded to look to Jesus — not just for the ultimate sacrifice at the cross, but for the daily relationship, He demonstrated with the Father. His death and resurrection allowed and made available to you this same relationship with the Father. When Jesus died, the veil was torn in two, and the boulders broke in half. Jesus' death provided our full access to the King of kings and Lord of lords.

Thank you, Jesus, for opening the door for this connection.

Prayer Starter: Jesus, thank you for being an example of how I can direct my heart toward God, focusing on You, Jesus, and my Heavenly Father with the Divine connection in the Holy Spirit that I can keep You, Jesus, as the compass of my life, a compass that always leads me to the Father!

The Cup: Salvation
Hebrews 9:14; 1 Peter 1:18–19; Leviticus 17:11

*J*esus' blood, from day one, was salvation. His D.N.A. (Divine and Natural Authority) was woven through and through with redemption. Every day of Jesus' life, His drive, endeavor, and heart was fed by salvation piercing through His blood. Every drop of His blood held salvation. Thus, every action, miracle, and experience demonstrates God's saving power. God showed us that when we accept Jesus, we are engrafted into the Tree of Life (the Lord Almighty) even in our humanness. He immediately infuses us with the blood of Jesus! Thus, once saved, our every desire is to lead others to the Savior.

Take this cup to remember the blood of Jesus flows in you and endues you with the power of Jesus!

Prayer starter: Thank you, Lord, that I am infused with the blood of Jesus because I am now engrafted into the Tree of Life. Jesus, I ask that You teach me how to live a life as You did; that my drive, my endeavors, and my heart will as well be fed by Your salvation blood piercing through me!

AFFIRMATIONS

Lord, help me to have the resolve to forgive, to hand myself over to the process of forgiveness, taking the pain of the humiliation and wrath, carrying the burden of forgiveness, and then nailing my unforgiveness to Your cross of forgiveness.

Day 10
The Bread: Devotion
John 4:34; Galatians 2:20; Romans 11:17-24

Jesus came to earth with an innate devotion and love for His Father. His birth father was the Lord, and the D.N.A. (Divine and Natural Authority) of the Almighty was in Jesus. Jesus demonstrated what devotion to our Father is. When Jesus went to the cross, He made it possible for us to call the Lord our Father! With every stripe (whipping) Jesus took, it was a cut into the Tree of Life (of God) that allowed us to be grafted into that tree! Jesus lived devoted to reaching this point so that all people would know the love of Jesus, the love of the Heavenly Father, and the love of the Holy Spirit.

Take this bread in remembrance of the loving devotion of Jesus to His Father and you.

Prayer Starter: Jesus, thank you that You demonstrated a level of devotion to Your Heavenly Father that far out measures any level of devotion I could have toward my earthly father. Yet, You made a way for me to give and receive this level of love and devotion from our Heavenly Father. Thank you for taking the stripes on Your back so that I would be able to be engrafted into the family of God!

The Cup: Focus
Proverbs 19:21; Ephesians 2:10; Jeremiah 29:11

*B*lood can be broken down into its finite elements. Each cell of blood can continually be broken down into smaller and smaller parts. Each minuscule element has a laser focus of what it is to do—its purpose. Just as with us! We are one person out of many people on Earth, yet we have laser focus and purpose and are infinitely important, needed, and wanted by God! Jesus shed every ounce of His holy blood at the cross to cover every one of us, including you, when you accept Him. Every drop focused on every one of us, on you! Throughout Jesus' life, every heartbeat that pumped each cell of His holy blood around His whole body had focus, purpose, love, compassion, and exponentially more that flowed in and through Him, driving and empowering Him to do everything He did.

Take this cup in remembrance of Jesus' focused blood that He shed at the cross for you. Ask the Lord to fill you with a focused level of flow in your life that continually drives you forward—closer and closer to the Lord—and also helps you focus on *His* heart, will, desires, and purpose, not only on yours.

Prayer Starter: Lord, I ask You to fill me with a focused level of flow in every area of my life that continually drives me forward, closer, and closer to You Lord, and helps me focus on Your heart, will, desires and purpose in every area of my life. I want to do Your will for my life; my life is Yours, Lord; do with me what You desire!

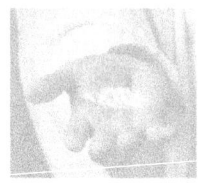

Day 11
The Bread: Tangible
Psalm 37:4–6; Romans 1:19–20; Psalm 34:8; Matthew 26:26

*J*ust as tangible as this cracker is in our hands, so is how tangible Jesus is, God is, and the Holy Spirit is! Feel the cracker touching you, see it in your hand, smell it, move it in your hand; you know it is there, and in a moment, you will taste and see that the Lord is good (Psalm 34:8).

Jesus commanded His disciples to take and eat the bread that represented His body (Matthew 26:26). We are doing the same while taking Holy Communion; we take the bread and eat it, representing Jesus' body sacrificed for us. Jesus' body died and was resurrected for us. Jesus going to the cross is as real as the cracker in your hand! Jesus commanded us to take this communion in remembrance of Him. Jesus is real; what He did and is doing is real! Tangible! Communion is not just a ritual; it is a daily reminder of how tangible the Godhead is. They are not somewhere out there; rather, they are right here, just as this cracker is right here in your hand.

Prayer Starter: Lord, as I eat this bread/cracker, I feel it, taste it, smell it; let it be that way for me with all You are. Lord, help me to experience You throughout every moment of my day tangibly. Jesus, thank you for being in me by the power of the Holy Spirit and working through me in tangible ways.

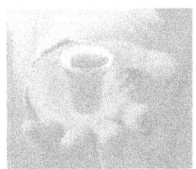

The Cup: Connection
Hebrews 9:14; Leviticus 17:11; John 20 & 21

*B*lood – nothing exists without the blood! We are made in the image of our Heavenly Father in every way. So, He too has blood coursing through His body, and Jesus had God's blood coursing through His body. Jesus poured every minuscule cell of His Divine and human blood out at the cross. This sacrifice allowed Jesus to make the connection between the Divine and our human (earthly) form. When Jesus was resurrected, God "filled again" Jesus' body with DIVINE blood so that Jesus could return to Heaven. God did this to demonstrate that we, too, will be resurrected with Divine blood and will tangibly be in a body in the heavenlies. Jesus showed us when He walked, talked, ate, moved that He had no limitations for 40 days with only Divine blood in Him, and we too will have this! We will not just be a wandering spirit without a body!

Take this cup in recognition of the Divine connection you have to God through Jesus' sacrifice on the cross! God's D.N.A. (Divine and Natural Authority) was in Jesus, who shed His blood so that you would be engrafted into the family of God through His blood. You are divinely connected to your Heavenly Father. All power and authority in the blood of Jesus flows in you, through you, and is connected via God's Holy Spirit in you.

Prayer Starter: Jesus, thank you for emptying Your earthly body of its holy and human blood so that I can have this connection to the Father. As well as for walking on Earth for 40 days with only holy blood, demonstrating that I will not just be a wandering spirit when I die, but I will be given a new body filled with holy blood just as Jesus was.

Day 12
The Bread: The Word of God
Galatians 5:24; Mark 8:35; Galatians 2:20; Hebrews 1:3

With a word, God formed everything. All that we know as well as all that we do not know. With a word, Jesus came to Earth. When God speaks, every utterance is filled with purpose and is carried out 100 percent of the time and with 100 percent accuracy! God designed the plan to bring Jesus to Earth to live, demonstrate, and save us. Jesus was 100 percent human and 100 percent Divine and made in the image of God. God sent Himself in the form of Jesus to redeem us back from the clutches of Satan. It was God's demonstration of what authority we as His children have on Earth. Jesus demonstrated that we must die just as He did "in our flesh"; we must die to our flesh daily so we can be raised in God's Divine authority just as Christ was. Only then will we see that we will do even more incredible things as we fulfill God's purpose on Earth.

Take the bread, focus your thoughts and attention on God's words spoken over you. God has given you words, His Word, and revelations that are filled with purpose and will be carried out with 100 percent accuracy, 100 percent of the time as you follow in the footsteps of Jesus and die daily to your flesh/self.

Prayer Starter: Lord, I ask that You bring to my remembrance those words You have spoken over me, the words You have illuminated to me in Your Word so that I can stand on Your purpose and call for my life. Help me die daily to my flesh/self and rise up in the authority You have given me in Jesus and imitating His character.

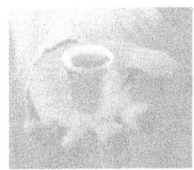

The Cup: Revelation
Ephesians 2:4–10; John 14:26, 15:26, 17

*J*esus came to reveal our authority on Earth; for 30+ years, Jesus showed and revealed to us our authority. Jesus revealed and demonstrated God's love, mercy, grace, healing, and sacrifice just to be in relationship with us. All of this was in Jesus' Divine blood and was transforming His human blood. At the cross where Jesus shed all His blood (both Divine and human), He shed it so that when we accept Him, His blood will be transfused into us (our new birth). Our transfusion of Divine blood covers us and strengthens our human blood. When Jesus was resurrected, God refilled Him with 100 percent Divine blood, revealing to us that we too will return to Divine blood only, in a body, just as Jesus did. As we die daily to the desires of this world, our transfusion of Divine blood replicates in our DNA and takes us from glory to greater glory and authority to greater authority!

Drink and remember how much God loves you. He sent Himself as JESUS to die for you and to infuse you with His blood, and then Jesus returned to Heaven. God sent His Holy Spirit to live and dwell in you so that you would have His power and authority residing in you and working in and through you. There is NO GREATER LOVE than the Father's love for you!!!

Prayer Starter: God, thank you for loving me so much that You not only sent Yourself to me as Jesus, but You sent Your Holy Spirit to live within me, dwelling in me so that I have Your power and authority living and working in and through me. I love You, Lord, and thank you for Your love for me!

Day 13
The Bread: Flesh/Body Submission
James 4:7; 1 Corinthians 9:26–27; Galatians 5:16–17; John 17:16

*J*esus was born into a body to be here on earth; however, He knew His authority over His flesh/body. It submitted to Him. As Jesus went into ministry, He demonstrated His authority over man's flesh/body. By a word or action, He healed and raised the dead, walked on water, translated, and sacrificed His flesh/body so that we can have the connection to the Father that Jesus has. Jesus demonstrated for us through His life, death, and resurrection what authority we have and how we are to beat our flesh/body into submission with the help of the Holy Spirit, in the blood of Jesus, and in obedience to our Heavenly Father. We are *in* this world, but not *of* this world (John 17:16). When we allow our flesh to rule, we have forgotten which world we are from! Jesus taught us how to keep our flesh/body in submission to our God-given, Jesus-bought, and Holy Spirit-enforced authority!

Take this bread to remind yourself of what Jesus taught and showed you as a reminder of your authority over your flesh/body. As you take this bread, commit to sacrificing your flesh as Jesus did on the cross.

Prayer Starter: Jesus, help me to do as Galatians 5:16 says. To walk by the Spirit so that I will have the power and authority NOT to gratify the desires of my flesh. Teach me, Lord, how to do as 1 Corinthians 9:27 says that I discipline my body and keep it under control. I ask this because I do not want to be disqualified, Lord, from what You have called me to do!

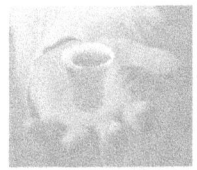

The Cup: Cleansing
1 Peter 1:18–19; 1 Corinthians 6:19–20; 2 Corinthians 5:17; 1 John 1:9

The blood of Jesus cleanses us! Before we were born again (when we accepted Jesus and recognized He died on the cross and rose again for us), our blood was tainted, stained, human through and through; this all changed when we were born again. Instantaneously, the blood Jesus shed at the cross for us was transfused into us. The blood we now have is human, yes, but it is also Divine; we were bought with a price that Jesus paid. His blood cleanses us from all unrighteousness (1 John 1:9); everything before that is under His blood. Now, the cleansing continues by us renewing our mind and the relationship building with the Godhead by realizing our authority, removing demons, changing patterns and habits, etc., that we had before our new birth. This process leads us closer and closer to our blood being cleansed, making us more Divine and less human, thus being continually transformed into the image of Christ.

Take this cup in remembrance of the blood Jesus shed and thank Jesus and the Holy Spirit for the continual cleansing process you are in so that you can do as Jesus did and even more, thus fulfilling your purpose.

Prayer Starter: Jesus, thank you for filling me with Your Divine blood that cleanses me from all unrighteousness. My past, even yesterday, is under the blood when I repent and return to You. I ask for Your help, Holy Spirit, to remove anything in me that hinders my ability to be Christ-like. Reveal to me, Lord, how to walk out the cleansing that Jesus' blood has done so that I can fulfill Your purpose for me.

Day 14
The Bread: Discipline
Matthew 6:33; James 1:5; 3:17; Jeremiah 33:3; 1 Thessalonians 5:16–18

Jesus was very disciplined. His focus on the Father's will was His priority. He was always ready and right where He needed to be, even if it was not what others' expectations and desires were. Jesus was disciplined to put God before Himself—He prayed to align His will and plan with God, get strength and wisdom, and be prepared for what would come. It is written that throughout Jesus' life, He would pray before every next move and the next day of interactions with people. We see this even during the last time when Jesus prayed in the Garden of Gethsemane. The most challenging assignment was before Him—dying for our sake on the cross. Jesus went into prayer, asking three times for the cup to pass, three times dying to himself saying, "Not my will but Yours, Lord." God gave Jesus the strength and resolve to face what would come. Jesus conquered death and resurrected.

Take this bread in remembrance of the discipline of going to God in prayer first to get the wisdom, strength, and resolve to conquer in your life!

Prayer Starter: Jesus, thank you for setting an example for me of how important it is to pray to our Father for direction, guidance, insight, and strength for everything I need. Jesus, You demonstrated in the Garden of Gethsemane that I line up my will with God's will when I pray. Help me, Holy Spirit, always remember to go to God in prayer before everything I do.

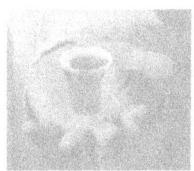

The Cup: Forgiveness
1 John 1:7; John 3:17, 12:47;
Psalm 25:8-15, 32:8

*J*esus' blood covers a multitude of sins. Too often, we condemn ourselves or listen to "demonic" voices whispering, "We missed it, we failed, we're unforgivable." The lies/word curses are endless. We neglect or forget to pray, get mad, curse, or yell at someone. Whatever "sin," big or small, causes us to feel embarrassed, dirty, or like a failure, so we believe the lies and run away from God because we think His call to repentance is based on shame, guilt, and punishment. Jesus did not choose to endure the whole process of dying on the cross to condemn us. No, He did it for our forgiveness! Jesus lived as a human; although He was sinless, He saw and lovingly dealt with every sin imaginable around Him. There is **NOTHING** we can do that will shock Jesus—He has seen it all! He still died and shed His blood to forgive us and cover us! Do not let the enemy's lies tell you any different. Jesus has a better way; He desires you to go to Him, repent, and be forgiven—but do not stop there! Ask Jesus how to walk holy in that area. He will teach you and guide you. He came to save us, not condemn us!

As you take the cup, focus on Jesus, talk to Him about where you feel that you are missing the mark. Repent, ask Jesus to forgive you, and thank Him for teaching you how to walk as He walked in those areas in your life. His blood, represented by the juice in the cup, represents how He lovingly covers a multitude of sins and how He has a better way that He wants to teach you.

Prayer Starter: Jesus, I am so grateful that Your blood covers my sins so that God does not hold them against me. So, I come to You, Jesus, to repent, renounce, and ask for forgiveness and guidance so that I can rejoice. You teach me through Your Word that the Holy Spirit guides me into all understanding, and God is always watching and making sure that I am where I need to be in His plan. Help me, Jesus, to be holy as You are holy!

AFFIRMATIONS

There is NO GREATER LOVE than the Father's love for me!!

I can be like Jesus and be disciplined to put God before myself – I pray as He prayed to align my will and plan with God, get strength and wisdom, and be prepared for what will come.

Notes

Day 15
The Bread: Repentance
Romans 3:23, 6:23, 12:2; 1 John: 7:9

Jesus cares about the little things. We know for the "big sins" we must come to Jesus to repent, but how often for the "little things"? Usually, at best, we may say, "Sorry Jesus!" or we just ignore them. Oh, how this hurts Jesus, just as the small, sharp points of His crown of thorns did as they pierced the thin skin on His head, digging through and to His skull. He shed His blood for even those "little sins."

Jesus' wounds heal miraculously. Pray that Jesus will renew and give revelation for new ways of thinking, being, and acting that will transform you as you turn your life over to Jesus, your Savior.

Take this bread now as a covenant reminder of what Jesus did and does for you.

Thank Jesus for the forgiveness of your repented sins in His name.

Prayer Starter: Lord, help me! Holy Spirit, guide me and reveal to me the ways I pierce Jesus' brow with a thorn; bring me to a place of repentance. Not condemnation or shame, but a genuinely repentant heart so the blood that pours from the wounds will cover, heal, and restore me.

The Cup: Power
Matthew 26:28; Revelation 12:11

Jesus is saying, "there is more power in one drop of My blood than all the waters combined on the face of the Earth and in the depths of it! And I shed <u>every single drop</u> of My blood for you! Oh, how I seek for you to understand the power you have. I left you all My power plus that which was in reserve within Me. My blood, My power can't die because it is mixed with the Divine eternal blood of our Heavenly Father!"

Imagine and understand that Jesus' blood has continued to grow exponentially in greater power as the battle looms ahead will require greater power. Jesus already provided the power and authority to trample the enemies, to save the lost, heal the sick, and to fear nothing in our pursuit to fulfill His purpose and bring all of God's children back to the Father. Jesus is just waiting for us to tap into the available power.

Take this cup as an agreement with Jesus to tap into His blood and the power it holds to the fullest capacity so you can constantly stay connected to the source—Jesus.

Prayer Starter: Lord Jesus, forgive me for negating the power of Your blood, for doubting the power, thinking I needed more and more of it when all I need is one drop. Help me, Lord Jesus, to recognize You have given me the power to do even greater things than have been seen to date, and all it requires is one drop of Your blood. Thank you for having covered me with Your blood. I tap into YOUR power now!

Day 16
The Bread: Brazen
John 5:19–23, 14:12; Acts 2:37

*W*ebster's dictionary defines the word brazen[3] as shameless boldness. Jesus embodied this! Jesus was shameless, knew who He was, who His Father was, what He believed and knew His purpose, and He was bold in doing God's will. Everything about Jesus was a very loud, brassy gong in the senses of His opposition. Jesus' words and actions were cutting, piercing, and destructive to the enemy's lies and the religious mindsets, all while life-giving, sustaining, and freedom to all who needed forgiveness, freedom, and salvation. Jesus only did what He saw His Father do (John 5:19–23). Jesus came so we would see what we are to do on Earth—to be brazen as Jesus was and is.

Prayer Starter: Lord Jesus, I take this bread in remembrance and thankfulness of the legacy of brazenness You left me. I'm determined not just to do what You, Jesus, did, but greater (John 14:12). As I take this bread, I commit to be shamelessly bold for You, Jesus. With Your strength and help, I will be confident to step out and boldly proclaim the truth! To embody all that You, Christ, lived, died, resurrected, and ascended for. Thank you for sending me the helper, the Holy Spirit. Amen!

---

[3] *https://www.merriam-webster.com/dictionary/brazen*

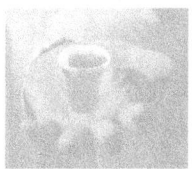

The Cup: Renewal
John 15:1-17

*J*ust as the tree flows with sap and nutrients, so does the blood of Jesus. Jesus' blood flows through us every day, renewing us. We are grafted into the tree of Life and fed by the powerful blood of Jesus that continually renews, heals, restores, and sets us free to be who God created and called us to be. You have the anointing of the Lord, Jesus, and God's Holy Spirit flowing through you because of the life-giving POWER of the blood of Jesus.

Take this cup in remembrance of the blood Jesus shed to open heaven's doors (the bark of the tree) to connect with God (the tree) and allow us to be grafted in and eternally fed by the sap (power and anointing) of God.

Thank you, Jesus, that Your blood seals my grafting in for eternity!

Prayer Starter: Jesus, you took the cuts in your back so that there would be a place for me to be engrafted into the tree of Life/God's Kingdom. Because of you, Jesus, I am restored, renewed, healed, and set free. By doing this, Jesus, you made a way for me to receive the sap/power and anointing that empowers me to be who God called me to be.

Day 17
The Bread: Anointing
Luke 8:45–46; Acts 1:8

Place the cracker on a piece of paper for a few minutes. You will see that although the cracker looks dry, hard, and not alive, there is life teeming in it. There are oils released that stain the paper. So too with the body of Jesus Christ. The anointing that was on and in Jesus, the Holy Spirit, His D.N.A. (Divine and Natural Authority) all flowed in, though, and out of Him. It was often unseen to the natural eyes but felt by the Spirit. No matter where Jesus went, the oil of anointing left its imprint. Even His dry, hard, dead body left a mark and an anointing that continues to flow. When He resurrected then ascended, He passed to us this same anointing through the Holy Spirit, and we are to leave an impact wherever we go. The oil of anointing can and will touch all who come in contact with it, just as it did with Jesus!

Take this bread in remembrance of the anointing that Jesus gave you access to when He died and rose for you. Ask God to use you to leave an imprint of Jesus everywhere you go. If you feel that your "oil of God's anointing" is low or not exuding from you to the level God desires, ask the Holy Spirit to teach you how to access the full measure of the anointing God has already provided you in the Holy Spirit.

Prayer Starter: Lord Jesus, I am seeking You to show me how to live my life, leaving an imprint of Your anointing everywhere I go. Holy Spirit, overflow in me with Your presence so that the "oil of God's anointing" will exude out of me and make a difference in the lives of all whom I encounter.

The Cup: Newness of Life
Romans 6:3–11; Acts 2:38

The blood of Jesus has the power for newness of life. However, the only way we can appropriate this newness of life is to die to self as Jesus did on the cross, be drained of all our unsaved, worldly blood through repentance. Then Jesus, who was our sacrifice for our forgiveness, will cleanse us and transfuse us with His blood—the blood He shed at the cross. His blood carries His D.N.A. (Divine and Natural Authority). We are now born again and have full access to the Divine and the natural, with the full authority granted to us by the blood of Jesus. We are now returned as a son/daughter of the Most High, God Almighty! Additionally, this opens the door for the <u>full measure</u> of the Holy Spirit to take residence in us. We are recreated by the D.N.A. of Jesus' blood which opens the door for the Holy Spirit to bring all of God/the Divine in full measure and power in us here on Earth!

As you drink from the cup, give thanks that you are a new creation in Jesus; that the blood He shed has washed away the tainted, unsaved, worldly blood, and you have been washed clean. Meditate on the full measure of the Divine and natural authority you now have since Jesus' blood has washed you. Jesus' D.N.A. is rewriting your earthly DNA, and the Holy Spirit has open access for you to all the power in Heaven and on Earth.

Prayer Starter: Thank you, Jesus, for newness of life and for the power and authority You have given me in Your D.N.A. Holy Spirit, continue to transform me from the inside out so that I can be made clean and walk moment by moment in the image of Christ.

Day 18
The Bread: No Condemnation
Romans 8:1

Romans 8:1 tells us, "There is now no condemnation for those who are in Christ." The enemy condemned the pure, innocent, blameless lamb of Christ who had no sin and had done no wrong. Our loving, compassionate, filled with grace and mercy, determined and focused Savior who was filled with destiny, purpose, and was on a mission to save the lost, stolen, kidnapped children of the God Almighty, took this all for us when He sacrificed His body, took the condemnation on Himself, was nailed to the cross, died, and was buried. But once He took the power and authority from Satan, Jesus rose victorious!

Take this bread in remembrance that Satan, his demons, and other humans (unredeemed and redeemed) have no authority to condemn us because Jesus took it all at the cross! Only Jesus can convict us, and when He does, we will repent and be washed clean; then He instantly renews our right standing with God.

Prayer Starter: Lord Jesus, thank you for taking on what I deserved so that I can be forgiven and not live in condemnation, but rather in the freedom and holiness that You paid for. Help me to walk in the confidence that no one has the authority to condemn me. You defeated the condemner's vile attacks and destroyed their power at the cross. Thank you, Jesus!

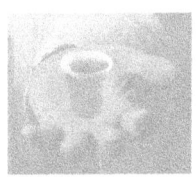

The Cup: Unrecognized Power
Luke 1:34–35; Matthew 1:20; Ecclesiastes 4:12; Isaiah 7:14

God himself sent his Holy Spirit to enter Mary and embed Himself in the form of Jesus. Miraculous God Himself hidden in Mary's womb. The power of the D.N.A. (Divine and Natural Authority) in the blood of Jesus was Divine, hidden in human form, as it still is in us. No one could recognize any difference; to them, He had the same blood as everyone else. But there was unrecognized Divine power in Jesus' blood. Before Jesus' crucifixion and resurrection, people knew He had power, but they could not truly recognize what was flowing through His veins. At the cross, Jesus poured out every ounce of this divine power that (God) has for us, to redeem us, cover us, and to transfuse us with this same power that still goes unrecognized not only by others but by all of us. The D.N.A., which is the blood of God and Jesus, flows through our veins, providing the one-two punch in addition to God's Holy Spirit who lives in us. We have the three-strand cord of power in us God, Jesus, and the Holy Spirit.

Drink from this cup in remembrance of the power Jesus gave you when He shed His blood for you, how His blood covers you and empowers you, along with God's Holy Spirit living inside of you, which provides you with unlimited power.

Prayer Starter: God, You came to Earth as a baby just so that You could fulfill Your promise in Isaiah 7:14. By Your Holy Spirit, You entered and created within Mary Yourself in the form of a human— Jesus. Just as I must accept You into me, so did Mary. As well, just as Mary had no real idea what it all meant, so it is true with me. Help me, Jesus, realize what power I have because God my Father, You, and God's Holy Spirit live within me. Through Your Holy Spirit, You remain in me for eternity.

# Day 19
The Bread: Connection
1 Timothy 3:16; John 14:6; 1 John 4:19

Hold the cracker, look at it, and ask the Holy Spirit to help you supernaturally feel a depth of connection to the real, tangible Jesus you serve. If you are using the mini-saltines, focus on the five holes—2 holes for the hands, 2 for the feet, and the middle one for His side where He was pierced. See the jagged edges of the cracker; this represents the crown of thorns and is symbolic of Jesus' shredded body from the whipping that sliced open His skin. The bubbled/raised areas represent the swelling in His body and the love that overwhelmed and bubbled up in Him for us. A love that drove Him on to persevere the agonizing and unbearable pain. Jesus IS as real as this cracker you see in your hand; He did all of this for you! Press into the realization that Jesus is real as you hold and take the bread! All He did, both Divine and natural, are as real as the cracker you hold in your hand! The crucifixion, death, and resurrection ARE real! Unconditional love, mercy, grace, compassion, and healing—ALL REAL! This cracker represents God embodied as Jesus who came to Earth to live with you, taught you, saved you, redeemed you, and gave you eternal life. You are connected to your Heavenly Father without limits because of the finished work of Jesus!

Take this bread, acknowledging the real, authentic, Divine God you serve, love, obey and embody—the one who first loved you while you were a sinner. Take this bread and eat it in remembrance of Jesus, the real and true and tangible Savior sent by God, to be God among us!

Prayer Starter: Lord, help me! Holy Spirit, guide me and reveal to me the ways I pierce Jesus' brow with a thorn. Bring me to a place of repentance. Not condemnation or shame, but a genuinely repentant heart so the blood that pours from Your wounds will cover me, heal me, and restore me.

The Cup: Superhighway Flow
Romans 12:2; 1 Peter 1:3–5; Matthew 28:18–20

At our new birth, Jesus infused/transfused His D.N.A. (Divine and Natural Authority) into us within the vehicle of His blood. Ever since, He has been driving the superhighway of our body, down to the rough terrain of the unknown, hidden paths, making them clean, unobstructed, and functional. Every moment of every day, we are renewed in every way, as Jesus' blood transports the Good News in and carries out for destruction the debris, the hindrances, anything that blocks the flow. Thus, the superhighway is wide open, unhindered, and acceleration is ever-increasing, opening the transportation of God's anointing, purpose, destiny, plan, and POWER to go and touch every cell (person), organ (nation), and body (world).

The blood of Jesus that this cup represents flows through us so we can transport what is in us to the whole body (world) just as Jesus still does today, transforming the body (world), organ by organ (nation by nation) and cell by cell (person by person).

Take the cup in remembrance of how the blood of Jesus is working through you first to transform you, then to overflow out of you for the world to be transformed.

Prayer Starter: Jesus, thank You for cleaning me out/transforming me so that YOU can flow unhindered through me to others, this nation, and this world. I am so grateful that I am being transformed day-by-day, moment-by-moment, into one who can serve You and fulfill Your purpose for my life.

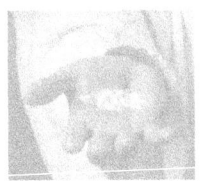

Day 20
The Bread: Priorities
Matthew 26:39; Hebrews 4:15; Mark 1:21-45

Throughout the life of Jesus, we see that he would separate Himself from the world to spend time with God in prayer. It did not matter what was going on, big or small; Jesus would go to God. He was praying and getting into alignment with the will of His Father; this was especially evident in regards to the crucifixion when He asked God to take the cup from Him, yet not His will but God's will (Matthew 26:39). Jesus put God first in His life, time, thoughts, words, actions, will, and ways. By doing this, Jesus remained pure amid a sinful world. Jesus did not achieve complete purity with no sin ever in His life by His strength alone. No, He struggled with all the issues we do because He was human! (Hebrews 4:15). But He demonstrated the importance of putting God first, knowing how to stay in the will of the Father, and how to handle our life without sin.

We often say or think, *but my life is so busy and hectic*; well, so was Jesus'. Think about it. He had twelve guys with Him constantly; people followed Him everywhere. He was a type of busy we do not comprehend! (A prime example is in Mark 1:21-45. Notice how many times the word "immediately" is used and how in-demand Jesus was). Yet, He knew the importance of time with His Father, as seen in verse 35 in the middle of Mark 1:21-45.

Prayer Starter: Lord, I do not want to neglect the essential part of making it in life, spending time with You, the Author and Finisher of my life. Your son needed You, and so do I! Forgive me for thinking I have too much to do to put You first. None of that will take priority over You, God! Help me learn how to fellowship with You continually to keep You in first place in my life.

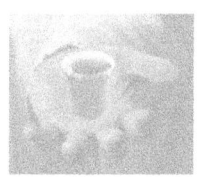

The Cup: Authority
Galatians 2:20; 1 Corinthians 6:19–20; Proverbs 3:5–6

This cup represents the blood of Jesus. Every day when taking communion, we do it to remind ourselves that Jesus' blood covers us. He shed every ounce of His blood for us! We were transfused with His blood when we were born again. Jesus' D.N.A. (Divine and Natural Authority) is infused into our blood, cells, and nuclei. When those cells replicate, they replicate with Jesus' D.N.A., not the RNA[4] (Regular Natural Authority). Included in the D.N.A. is the written code of how Jesus thought, spoke, and functioned—His anointing, power, and dominion—everything about Him. Jesus' D.N.A. comes directly from His Father, the Lord God Almighty. Now we have access because of being born again and infused with Jesus' D.N.A. Replication of those genes occurs as we go deeper in understanding through the guidance of the Holy Spirit.

By taking this cup during communion daily, we remember the D.N.A. that is replicating by renewing our mind to fulfill God's purpose for us!

Prayer Starter: Jesus, I am so grateful that I have been transfused with Your blood and that Your D.N.A. flows through my veins, making me more like You and transforming me into Your image.

---

[4] *According to DNA From the Beginning (http://www.dnaftb.org/26/), RNA was the first genetic molecule and it can function on its own, but is very unstable because it is a single strand; DNA is much more stable and a better form to pass genetic information accurately. RNA versus DNA is interesting if you think about it: we can function without God, but we are unstable. However, once we accept Jesus, we become a double strand, and we are like the DNA that is more stable for passing on genetic (God's genetic) information.*

Replicating You in me; the way You thought, spoke, and functioned. I am so honored that You gave me the Holy Spirit to be the glue that holds me divinely connected to You.

Notes

Notes

Day 21
The Bread: Your Focus
Colossians 3:2; Psalm 1:1–6; Luke 6:45

*W*e live in a world full of distractions, to-do lists, and disturbances that pull us away from focusing on Jesus, which is something that Jesus remembers vividly while He was here on Earth. Praying alone and taking communion daily before anything else is a way to purposely focus on Jesus so that amid life's chaos, we can focus our minds on Him. Jesus and the Holy Spirit teach us about all God has and is providing for us and how who we are in Christ will cause us to stand out. Thus as we remain faithful to Jesus, He will hone our level of focus and our attention and desires on His plans and purposes. Do not be moved by the accolades, credit, and recognition from others. Human recognition is shifting sand; today, they may love you and tomorrow curse, despise, and hinder you from your intimate relationship with Jesus.

Prayer Starter: Lord, my life is overwhelmed with distractions, to-do lists, and ungodly disturbances that keep pulling me away from the intimate relationship I desire to have with You. As I take this time to pray and communion with You, Lord, illuminate and direct me in how to handle all the demands in my life: what to let go of, what to attend to, and what to turn over to You. Thank You for this laser focus.

The Cup: Family
John 1:12–13; Romans 8:14–17; Ephesians 2:11–22

In the natural, our DNA[5] that contains our genes can be USED to determine who we are genetically related to—who our "family" is.[6] In the Divine, this is true as well. When we accept Jesus, His blood is infused into us, and our DNA is marked and can be identified spiritually as belonging to the family of Christ! We are joint-heirs in the Kingdom of God (Romans 8:14–17). Our engrafting into God's family is all-inclusive; we are now given all "D"ivine and "N"atural "A"uthority in the Heavenlies and here on Earth.

Take this cup in remembrance of the blood Jesus shed to cover you, designate you as family, and engraft you into God's family where you are co-heirs with Christ.

Prayer Starter: Thank you, Lord, for creating a deeper depth of connection through the bonds of the D.N.A. (Divine and Natural Authority) in the blood of Jesus that was shed for me!

---

[5] ***Interesting fact:*** *Did you know that at the base-pair level your genome is 99.9 percent the same as all of the humans around you - but in that 0.1 percent difference are many of the things that make you unique?*
https://www.genome.gov/dna-day/15-ways/human-genomic-variation

[6] ***For more information, check out:***
http://www.differencebetween.net/science/difference-between-dna-and-genes/

Day 22
The Bread: Makes a Way
1 Peter 1:18–19; Matthew 27:51; Hebrews 10:19–22

*J*esus made a way for us to connect with God personally. In the Old Testament, priests would die instantly in the presence of God if they entered the Holy of Holies unclean. Jesus, the only person who was spotless, sacrificed Himself so that we could enter the Holy of Holies unhindered. Jesus made this possible when the veil was torn in two, and the boulder was split in half. Open access into the Holy of Holies was provided to us as every drop of Jesus' blood left His body. He covered all our sins that we asked for forgiveness of and made us pure and holy like Him so we can come before God.

It is now God in the form of the Holy Spirit who lives in us (the same Holy Spirit who lived in Jesus) and is the power that gives us the ability to create, change, direct, and have complete authority in the spirit realm. This power flows through us to fulfill God's mission and plan for our life! Take this bread in remembrance of the open door Jesus created so that you have complete connection with your Father God.

Prayer Starter: Lord, thank You for sending Your son, Jesus, to die for me so that I can boldly and confidently come into Your presence. Thank You, Lord, for sending the Holy Spirit, the same one who worked in and through Jesus, so that I too can have power and the ability to create, change, direct, and have complete authority in the spirit realm. Help me to learn more about this so that I can fulfill Your plan for my life.

The Cup: The Blood is for the Redeemed
2 Corinthians 4:4; Luke 23:34; Romans 1:18–20, 10:9–10

*T*hroughout the whole process of crucifixion, Jesus was shedding His blood in a violent and gruesome way. So, think about it; just one drop of Jesus' blood has the power to deliver us, heal us, cleanse us, and so much more—**just one drop**! There is no way all who were around, as Jesus' blood was pouring from His body, did not get splattered with even one drop of His blood! But it did not affect them because without the knowledge and understanding of who Jesus was and because of their outright rejection of Him, their unbelief, doubt, and hardened hearts, God's redemption that was available to them became null and void. Satan had blinded their hearts, minds, souls, ability to reason, and any conviction. Even Jesus said, "Forgive them, for they know not what they do" (Luke 23:34).

For the power and authority, redemption, healing, forgiveness, love, and so much more to flow through us, we must accept Jesus. Then all the power and authority in the blood of Jesus can transform us and restore us to sonship (daughter-ship), renewing our Heavenly passport. All with just one drop of His blood, and **yet** He floods us and covers us with His blood!

So, what are you not living in/doing/experiencing due to your doubt, unbelief, or lack of understanding of who your Father God is and what price Jesus paid for you?

Prayer Starter: Oh Lord, help me just as Jesus helped the boy with the unclean spirit in Mark 9. Even his father said, "I believe; help my unbelief!" Lord, I know and believe in the power of the blood of Jesus, even just one drop; but help my unbelief that hinders and even stops me from living and flowing in the power and authority, redemption, healing, forgiveness, love, and so much more that Jesus' blood provides for me.

Day 23
The Bread: Path
Psalm 16:11, 119:105; John 15:18; Galatians 5:24

Every aspect of Jesus' life from conception to His resurrection was a path for us to follow and understand. Beginning with conception, Jesus became a human when His Heavenly Spirit combined with God's Holy Spirit to conceive Him in Mary's womb. Our human body is formed within our mother's womb after our <u>dual</u> human (mother and father) egg and sperm merge. Then our Heavenly Spirit and God's Holy Spirit enter us, breathing life into us.

Every step of Jesus's life showed us the path to walk in complete authority, power, and dominion. How to treat others, interact with God, and how to minister. Even going through rejection, assaults against our character, being beaten and ridiculed, hung on a cross to die (hopefully only our flesh), and dying (to self). A process we must go through to live as Jesus lived! The death of our flesh, self, and earthly motives as Jesus did, and then resurrect as victorious over the death, lies, and the destruction Satan thought he had over us! This path was laid so we can be in obedience to God. The last thing Jesus did on Earth was He ascended in His redeemed Divine body to intercede for us to the Father. We, too, will ascend to join Jesus in our redeemed Divine body, fully reconciled to God!

Take this bread in remembrance of the path that Jesus laid out for you to reign and rule with full power, authority, and dominion here on Earth and in the spirit realm, just as Jesus did! God provided you with the full measure of the Holy Spirit when Jesus ascended; to live in you and fill you with all of Himself.

Prayer Starter: Lord, You planned even before creating the world who my parents would be. The exact earthly DNA I required to be who You needed me to be. Then when my time came, You breathed life into me. Thank You for sending Jesus to be a template of what I would have to go through, as well as giving me the hope of the glory of returning to You with my redeemed body to live with You forever. Holy Spirit, help me thoroughly understand what You know and have at my access if only I ask.

AFFIRMATIONS

- For the power and authority, redemption, healing, forgiveness, love, and so much more to flow through me, I must accept Jesus (as Lord of my life).
- It is now God in the form of the Holy Spirit who lives in me (the same Holy Spirit who lived in Jesus), and is the power that gives me the ability to create, change, direct, and have complete authority in the spirit realm. This power flows through me to fulfill God's mission and plan for my life!
- There is a process I must go through to live as Jesus lived. The death of my flesh, self, and earthly motives just as Jesus did, and then resurrect as victorious over death, lies, and the destruction Satan through he had over me!

Day 23
The Cup: Protection
Psalm 91; Hebrews 9:14; Exodus 12:13

The blood of Jesus is a hedge of protection that breaks the chains to this world, removes all iniquity and footholds of the enemy, is a shelter in the storm, and gives us authority, dominion, and power! That is some of the functions of the blood of Jesus—its redemptive properties that cover us to be not just in the presence of God, but for God to live within us through the Holy Spirit. We are sealed with the blood of Jesus, which confuses the enemy's plans; whatever fiery darts he shoots at us are deflected because the blood of Jesus covers us. We are protected, but this does not mean our life is a bed of roses, for the enemy is trying to attack and kill us. However, Jesus' blood declares that no matter what happens, we have victory! It angers Satan when He sees the blood of Jesus covering us because it reminds Him that Christ already defeated him. We are redeemed and will have eternity with God.

Take this cup in remembrance of and with gratitude for the protection you have because of what Jesus did for you. The blood of Jesus covers you and provides you with a hedge of protection from the fiery darts of the enemy.

Prayer Starter: Lord, I am protected by what Your Son, Jesus, did for me. I do not have to fear the enemy's attacks because You, Lord, are a hedge of protection surrounding me. The blood of Jesus covers me and does not allow the fiery darts of the enemy to penetrate and hurt me. I thank You, Lord, that when life is "hard," I can trust that You are with me in those attacks.

Notes

Day 24
The Bread: Understanding
Genesis 3:8; John 15:26, 17:20–26; Romans 8:9

𝒲e serve a God who does understand what we are going through. Yes, God is sovereign. He has every day of our lives numbered and knows what will happen. But God longed for fellowship with us as He had with Adam and Eve. He desired to redeem us from Satan's control. So, God sent Himself in the form of Jesus, His one and only Son, to walk with us, to fellowship with His humanity that He created. God knew Jesus would have to die so that His children would be redeemed and in right relationship with Him. Thus, Jesus lived, died, resurrected, and sits next to our Father God to advocate for us. But God still did not want to be separated from us, so He decided a connection needed to continue, not just be alongside His children but be **IN** His children; so He sent His Spirit—the Holy Spirit! The Holy Spirit came to reside in our redeemed body with God's full power and authority.

Take this bread in remembrance of all God has done due to His unconditional love for you, to be in fellowship, and to understand and be with you. To be **ONE** with you!

Prayer Starter: God, Your desire to be with me, in me, and a part of my life was the reason You did all You did. You wanted to know what it was like for me, so You sent Yourself as Jesus; You wanted to redeem me, so You hung Yourself/Jesus on the cross so that I could be one with You, and yet that was not enough. You still desired to be in me for the rest of time, so You came into me in the form of the Holy Spirit. Lord, help me to desire You with the same intensity as You desire me!

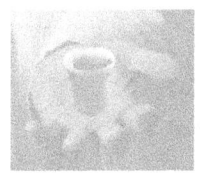

The Cup: Marks You
Revelation 1:5–6; 1 Timothy 6:15; Job 33:4; Acts 17:25

When we were born, we already had God's breath in our lungs, and we were marked by the Holy Spirit, just like when Jesus was born. Satan used Herod to try to kill Jesus, and even now, Satan uses whatever he can to try to kill us. We are the target of Satan's hatred for God. Jesus came to save us from this, to redeem us to God! It is the best gift God could give us, and all we must do is accept the gift of new birth by the blood of Jesus and His resurrection. We are born-again, so now the target on us has increased, the bounty for our life is increased by Satan because we now have what he will never have—Jesus' blood in us! Satan hates knowing we are covered by the blood of Jesus and are a child of the Most High, an heir with Christ. We are Satan's kryptonite! We have Jesus' D.N.A. (Divine and Natural Authority), and His blood covers us, protects us, and redeems us!

Take this cup in remembrance of how the blood of Jesus marks you as a child of the most-high God and Father and makes you an heir with Christ immediately. You do not have to wait until you get to Heaven to walk in the full measure of being an heir. God wants you to walk NOW as the king/queen you are! God is the KING of kings (us) and LORD of lords (us), making you royalty NOW because of what Jesus did for you!

Prayer Starter: Thank you, Lord, for Your breath in my lungs. Your breath of life and the gift of the Holy Spirit are what allow me to know You still have a purpose for me. When I accepted Jesus, was covered in His blood, and was redeemed, I became an heir with Christ and a king/queen and lord on this earth. I am Satan's kryptonite because of the blood of Jesus and Your Holy Spirit in me. Thank you, Lord, that no matter what happens in my life, I can know I am yours—something Satan can NEVER be!

Day 25
The Bread: Willing
Matthew 8:1–4; Philippians 2:6–8

*W*hatever the Father asked of Jesus from the beginning of time, Jesus was always willing. Jesus willingly came to Earth to live and die as a human and then be raised as Divine. When He walked and ministered on Earth, He often spent time praying and communing with His Father God. On one occasion, after teaching from the mountain, a man with leprosy[7] came to Jesus and humbly yet confidently said, "If you are willing, you can heal me!" He asked to be healed, but for Jesus to completely heal this man, He would not just perform an external healing. Instead, Jesus went to the root (internally) and cleansed this man. Jesus said, "I am willing," so He touched him, and the man was healed immediately.

Ask the Lord, "What is my leprosy?" Humbly come before the Lord and ask the Lord for healing (true deep healing) because Jesus **is willing**! Our human nature will cause us to tell of our healing to everyone. However, Jesus gave a key that is often missed. We are not to tell anyone until we have gone to the Lord for the repentance and cleansing process, so we will never be in bondage to that which manifested as leprosy. Jesus is willing to heal; we must be willing to do our part of the process.

Take this bread and meditate on how crucial it was for Jesus to be willing to do whatever God asked of Him. What is in your life that you can ask Jesus to help you be more willing in?

Prayer Starter: Jesus, thank you for being willing; willing to do all You did and continue to do. Holy Spirit, help me see what the

---

[7] **Leprosy:** *An outward manifestation of an internal issue.*

cause of my leprosy is. What outward manifestations point me to an internal issue that I must be willing to go to Jesus for healing. Jesus, I know You are eager to heal and restore me; help me to be willing to open up and let it go, to release it to You, even if I have held onto it for a long time. I will obey and go to the Lord and repent and be cleansed by Your blood, Jesus.

AFFIRMATIONS

- Lord, help me to desire You with the same intensity as You desire me!
- God, You are the KING of kings (me) and LORD of lords (me), making me royalty NOW because of what Jesus did for me!
- I am Satan's kryptonite because of the blood of Jesus and God's Holy Spirit in me. Thank you, Lord, that no matter what happens in my life, I can know I am Yours – something Satan can NEVER be!

Day 25
The Cup: Are You the One?
Luke 17:11–19

*A*re you the one who is living a life of leprosy? Where is all the internal turmoil externally manifesting? From a distance, we yell out to God to have mercy on us! Jesus tells us to come to Him—the High Priest, so we come (with our "posse" of those manifesting with leprosy as well). In the process, before we even get to Jesus, He has already healed us! We accepted the responsibility to come to Jesus, who died for us, shed His blood, and resurrected completely healed. The rest of our crew was healed as well because all of us came to Jesus. But they kept going in their half-healed way, whereas we are the only ones who have continued to pursue Jesus, thanking Jesus, giving Him all glory and praise. We devote ourselves to Jesus, sitting at His feet worshiping. Jesus then washes us 100% clean forever with the blood He shed for our redemption at the cross. Are you that one? Or have you been one of the ungrateful nine?

Regardless of which one you are, take this cup and first repent and come back; come back if you have been one of the ungrateful nine. Then, drink in remembrance with the one who came back so you can rejoice for your complete healing because of the blood of the high priest—Jesus.

Prayer Starter: Oh Jesus, forgive me for the areas in my life where I was like the ungrateful nine. You healed me, and I just went on my way, never acknowledging what you did. I repent and come back now. I will devote myself to You, Jesus; I will sit at Your feet worshipping You because You, Jesus, are worthy. You have done so much for me, and I am so grateful.

Journaling

What has God done for you? Write a gratitude list thanking Him for all He has done.

_____

_____

_____

_____

_____

_____

_____

_____

_____

_____

_____

_____

_____

Day 26
The Bread: Unhinged
Matthew 7:7, 27:51; Revelation 1:8, 3:8, 20

*B*efore Jesus, no one could enter the presence of God except the priests, and even then, only with a sacrifice. **But Jesus!** Jesus changed this for us! Jesus sacrificed Himself once and for all. The door that was closed to us is open because of all Jesus did to bear our iniquities. He picked up the cross (symbolizing the <u>door</u> that blocked us and separated us from God). Jesus was nailed to the cross, symbolizing He was now the door. When He died, it seemed Jesus was just another high priest who died and would be put in a tomb, and life would go on. **But Jesus** was not the same! He went and got the keys so that the door to God could never be closed and locked again. The door was taken off the hinges, allowing us full access to the Holy of Holies. Jesus resurrected with the keys to freedom for us!

Take this bread with a grateful heart that Jesus took every hindrance of fellowship with God off the hinges, allowing you OPEN ACCESS to God!!!!

Prayer Starter: Jesus, You came to Earth to become the doorway to an intimate connection with the Father. By dying, You ended the division between God and me. Jesus, as You stand and knock at the door of my heart if fear grips me when I open the door, I can remember You rose after dying on the cross. I give You full access to me so I can go into the Holy of Holies and have open access to God.

The Cup: You Are the Access Point
Psalm 139:13–16; Ephesians 1:3–16

*J*esus' blood makes it possible for the Holy Spirit to work in and through us.

When we were born, our Heavenly spirit came to earth along with the Holy Spirit. When our physical body was formed, God breathed our Heavenly spirit and His Holy Spirit into us inside our mother's womb, and we came to life. Our "personal" Heavenly spirit (our personality, quirks, ways, etc.) has control, while the Holy Spirit is with us but limited in power until we give our life to Jesus and become born again. At that point, the D.N.A. (Divine and Natural Authority) of Jesus is activated when we are washed in the blood. Then, the Holy Spirit freely manifests all the power and authority of God in and through us. You see, Jesus had to die, shed every drop of His blood, and the Holy Spirit had to leave His body so He could live in us. After three days, Jesus rose — completely Divine, and now God's Holy Spirit is free to have full access to all His children. Once we accept Jesus as Lord and Savior, His D.N.A. gives access to God's Holy Spirit to live and work in and through us. We are the access point for God to move in and on this earth as He did with Adam and Eve.

Take the cup in remembrance of the open-access God now has to you. When God sent you from Heaven to Earth, He placed His Holy Spirit in you when He breathed life into you. Oh, the angst He had being separated from you. Yet, oh, the joy He had when you accepted Jesus as your Savior and His Holy Spirit was then freed in you, which allowed God full access to you. He once again can live in you, walk with you, guide you, lead you, and direct you to fulfill His purpose for you in this world.

Prayer Starter: Oh Lord, I am so glad that by accepting Jesus, Your Son, I have unlocked the full power and authority You gave me by Your Holy Spirit. You knew me before You formed me in my mother's womb. You determined who I would be, what family I would be in, and breathed life into me. Help me learn who I am in Your eyes so that I can fulfill Your purpose in this world.

Psalm 139:13-16 (NIV)

13. For you created my inmost being; you knit me together in my mother's womb.
14. I praise you because I am fearfully and wonderfully made; your works are wonderful, I know that full well.
15. My frame was not hidden from you when I was made in the secret place, when I was woven together in the depths of the earth.
16. Your eyes saw my unformed body; all the days ordained for me were written in your book before one of them came to be."

Notes

Day 27
The Bread: Boldness in Confidence
Hebrews 13:6; Ephesians 3:12; Proverbs 11:2; James 4:10

*J*esus demonstrated to us throughout his life how we are to live with humble boldness due to God's opinion, calling, revelation, and understanding in our life. Jesus' confidence was found and established in His Father—our Father! Not in the opinions of man. Due to that, Jesus demonstrated and emulated a distinct level of boldness that set Him apart. <u>It was never arrogance, haughty pride, or hurtful disrespect, all of which only come from confidence in Satan, flesh, and self.</u> This confidence was demonstrated with boldness, exuded with authority, and caused Jesus to be honored and respected because He had power and completion of every word that proceeded out of His mouth. He accurately demonstrated every direction of our Father God.

Take this bread in remembrance that the boldness you want is only found in the deep confidence of who you serve and all His truths. God is living within you as the Holy Spirit, and His words and truths are demonstrated in and through you. You have Jesus to emulate and to redeem you; however, you must approach life and people with the same confidence you approach the throne of God!

Prayer Starter: Jesus, teach me to have the humble boldness You had, thus being confidently founded and established in You. Set me apart from those who have confidence in self, flesh, and Satan. Teach me, Holy Spirit, to be confident, bold, exuding the authority Jesus paid the price for me to have, all while humbly acknowledging You as the source of my confidence.

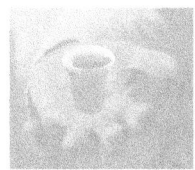

The Cup: Refreshing
James 1:17; John 4:13–14; Psalm 1:3

The blood of Jesus is a refreshing river of life that continually flows. It is made of healing and redemptive cells, power, and authority-infused elements, and every good and perfect gift from above. Jesus' blood flows within us, carrying all He is through every part of us. His blood covers us, cleansing us moment-by-moment as we repent and turn back to Him. His blood is protecting us from the enemy and the things of this world that seek to trap, ensnare, and condemn us. Jesus' blood has everything we need to be refreshed and strengthened and to have the humble, bold confidence in the Godhead alone!

Drink this cup in remembrance of all that Jesus' blood carries. It is the power in you to be bold (in the words and actions) and done through you by the Holy Spirit and manifested in the Earth. This river of life is refreshing you continually and will never run dry!

Prayer Starter: Thank you, Jesus, for what Your bloodshed has enabled me to learn, know, and understand as Your ever-flowing blood is in me, on me, and coming out of me!

Day 28
The Bread: Do Not Mourn
Ezekiel 24:16–18; 2 Corinthians 5:17; Galatians 2:20; 1 Peter 2:9

In Ezekiel 24:16–18, God told Ezekiel that He would take the delight of His eyes in one blow. But He was NOT to mourn; he could quietly groan but not publicly mourn. Ezekiel was to continue to move and press forward. When Jesus sacrificed Himself on the cross for our salvation and redemption, He opened the door for connection to our Father God. With this one blow, He destroyed the delight of our eyes. For Ezekiel, it was his wife; for us, it is our worldly life, the lusts of our flesh, the hunger for money, fame, recognition. Only you know what "delights" you have.

When you take this bread, you do it in remembrance as God told Ezekiel—do not lament, weep, or shed any tears. Do not mourn for the dead "delights." Do not show outwardly that you miss, are sad, regretting, sorry, or anything else for that which is dead. Who you were before Christ became your King, your Savior is dead! You are a new creation in Christ; old things have passed away!

Prayer Starter: Lord, remove from me those earthly, carnal delights that Jesus died for. Help me not to lament, weep, or shed any tears since my past is dead; not forgotten, but dead. It has no power nor authority over me.

The Cup: Priceless Pearls
Matthew 7:6; 2 Peter 2:22; Proverbs 1:1–7

Jesus' blood is sacred! He shed it for everyone to be born again, saved, sanctified, and redeemed, thus becoming a child of God! Salvation is meant for everyone. We must share and give everyone the opportunity to accept Jesus. However, many of us take for granted or mistakenly assume that the priceless pearls that were given to us by God, Jesus, and the Holy Spirit must also be given to everyone. In Matthew 7:6, Jesus tells us, "Do not give dogs what is sacred; do not throw your pearls to the pigs; if you do, they may (the dogs and the pigs) trample them under their feet, and turn and tear you to pieces!" What special, priceless pearls have you thrown to the pigs (the unclean, unsacred), which have then turned against you? The blood of Jesus is sacred, and dogs will eat and drink anything and demand more. What Jesus did for you when you accepted Him was He washed you clean. It was a sacred experience that set the stage for the pearls you will receive. Guard them; they are a gift from God your Father just for you.

As you take the cup, repent and ask God for forgiveness for any times, you may have thrown His precious pearls given especially to you to the dogs or pigs. Ask the Holy Spirit to help you to know what to hold close and what to give. Thank God for the pearls He has given you, for the ones to come, and make a promise to guard them, giving them out ONLY when He commands you to.

Prayer Starter: Lord, thank you for all the special gifts You have given me and the wisdom You have imparted to me. In my zeal and lack of understanding, many times, I have thrown these pearls to pigs and dogs that stomped on them or ate them and minimized the awesomeness of what You gave me. Forgive me, Lord, and help me recognize when I am to share and when I am to enjoy with You alone so I can grow in wisdom and understanding. Help me to trust that You will tell me when to share and when to dig deeper.

Journaling

Make a list of precious pearls God has given you.

_____

_____

_____

_____

_____

_____

_____

_____

_____

_____

_____

YOUR GOD-GIVEN DIVINE & NATURAL AUTHORITY

Continue Listing the Precious Pearls Here:

_____
_____
_____
_____
_____

Which of these did you share that were meant to be kept personal or vice versa?

_____
_____
_____
_____
_____
_____
_____
_____

Day 29
The Bread: Roots Out What is Destroying You!
Joshua 7; 1 Peter 2:24; Galatians 5:24; Romans 8:13; Revelation 1:18

In Joshua 7, the Israelites had been winning every battle, but they went to fight an easy battle and lost. Sin had entered the camp through one man and caused wrath that cursed Israel and caused defeat and death. Joshua could not understand what was happening, until God revealed it to him. Then God walked Joshua through the process of who and what the sin was. Once found, all Aikens family and anything connected to Him were killed, burned up, and a monument was built. God's anger ceased, and Israel became victorious again! Their honor was restored! Jesus did this for us! We allowed sin into our life, taking from this world what God told us not to take as it would destroy us. Jesus came and, being the sacrifice for us, took on the destruction we deserved. Yes, Jesus was killed; however, He defeated death by going to the grave and rising. For all of eternity, the Cross will signify our redemption from the sins that were destroying and even killing our life and our destiny.

Take this bread in remembrance and gratefulness that God shows you the sin in you and removes it. Jesus paid the price for you to be healed and restored to holiness. You, unlike Jesus, may not have to die physically; but you must die to sin, the things of this world and the lusts of the flesh.

Prayer Starter: Thank you, Jesus, for paying the price for me to be free from the wrath of God for what I have taken from this world and hidden in my heart. Holy Spirit, peel back the layers to those things that are destroying me and angering God. Restore my honor, God, in Your eyes, and help me look to You and not this world.

The Cup: The Blood of Jesus Peels Back the Layers
Joshua 7:14-23; Romans 6:6; 1 John 1:9; Ephesians 4:22-24, 30

The blood of Jesus flows through us when we belong to Him. Jesus desires us to be a pure and holy replica of Him to the honor of our Lord, King, and Father God. Jesus does not want us to hold on to anything that removes the protection He paid for. So just as God chose the tribe, clan, family, and man; until Aiken was chosen and the sin was revealed, God does this with us. Some call it the layers of the onion. God reveals to us those areas where we have hidden our sin, which is the root of the cause of our destruction, oppression and is the reason God's hand of protection had to be removed. But God does not do this to destroy us because He sent Jesus to be the final death and resurrection, resulting in our redemption. One of the keys to this that we often ignore or neglect is that all family, belongings, animals, finances, and clothing connected to Aiken had to be killed, burned up, and memorialized. But Jesus did that for us. What have you held on to from your sin that needs to be covered by the blood of Jesus? Ask the Holy Spirit to reveal it to you so you can allow the blood of Jesus to cover it and redeem it so God's anger will cease.

Take some time to talk to God and ask Him to reveal what you have within you that is grieving His Holy Spirit. Then repent, renounce your connection to them and ask Jesus to cleanse you of those things and wash you in His blood.

Prayer Starter: Lord, thank you for revealing to me those things that are grieving You. I repent for holding onto those things, those people, and the feelings/emotions. I renounce the control I have given it in my life, and I renounce the continuous harboring of it, thinking I was hiding it from You. I ask You, Lord, to forgive me, wash me in the blood of Jesus, and restore me to right standing with You! Now take the cup and rejoice in your restoration.

THE D.N.A. OF COMMUNION

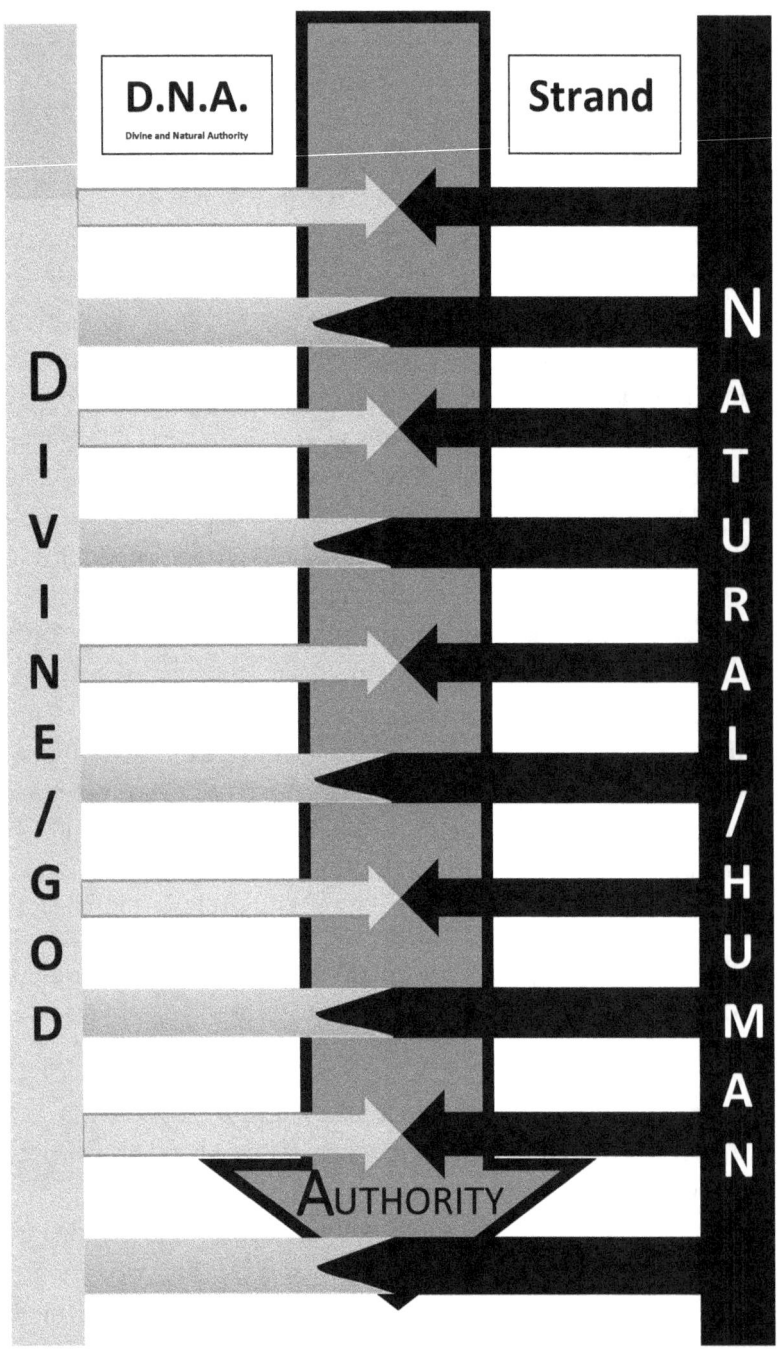

Notes

Day 30
The Bread: Making Bread
John 6:1-15, 25-59; 1 Corinthians 5:8

Jesus is the (unleavened) bread of life! We are the (leavened) bread that Jesus came to set free. Due to sin (yeast/leaven), we need a Savior without sin (yeast free/unleavened). In John 6, Jesus came to set the captives free, feed the lost, and quench their hunger for more. What goes into making bread?

<u>Flour, yeast, salt, and water.</u>
- **Flour** = made from the fruit of wheat—you; once planted, grown, harvested, threshed, winnowed, and crushed, you're primed for use.
- **Yeast** = Biblically, yeast is representative of sin. Because of the sin of Adam, you were born with yeast (with sin in you). Christ gave His body as the only way to remove the yeast and sanctify you. (Hebrews 10:10, 14)
- **Salt** = You are the salt of the earth; when salt loses its taste, God throws it away. Salt is a flavor enhancer. (Matthew 5:13)
- **Water** = Holy Spirit, purity, the blood of Jesus washes white as snow. (Ezekiel 36:25–26; John 3:5; 7:37–39)

Jesus saved you, and you became the bread He serves to continue to feed the hungry and lost and to satiate their hunger for Him. Take this bread and commit to do your part.[8]

Prayer Starter: Lord, help me understand each ingredient and the process You are taking me through to be the bread You need me to be. Lord, You created me with purpose and destiny. I want

---

[8] *https://www.compellingtruth.org/unleavened-bread.html*

to do my part in feeding Your sheep, bringing home the lost, and accurately utilize Your wisdom and knowledge in me to encourage their hunger for You and starve the desire for the things of this world. Do it in me, Lord, so I can be a vessel to help others as well.

Notes

Day 30
The Cup: All of You
Malachi 3:6–12; Romans 12:1; Mark 8:35

𝒯hese scriptures address tithes and offerings and are most often equated ONLY to money. Let Me show you, says the Lord, that I do not change. Still to this day, you turn away from My decrees and do not keep them. Return to Me, and I will return to you. You rob Me in tithes and offerings. I tell you to bring the WHOLE tithe into the storehouse so there will be food in My house. What do I want in My house? YOU! ALL OF YOU! I have given you life and life more abundantly. All I ask from you is your whole life! Even Jesus, My only Son, gave His whole life by literally dying, shedding all of His blood, and replanting it into the earth for a harvest of souls; and look what I did! I threw open the floodgates of Heaven and poured out so much blessing that there was not enough room to store it! And Jesus rose from the dead to eternal life! The crop/harvest is prevented from being devoured by the pest (Satan); the chains/shackles/destruction cannot stop your fruit, devour it, or take it before it is ripe. You are called blessed, and precious, and the best in the land. Yet you rob Me of your whole tithe—**YOU**!

Drink and remember the tithes and offerings Jesus gave.

Prayer Starter: Lord, You do not care about the money; You care about me. Father, forgive me for "tithing" my money, yet holding back myself the tithe You want. Lord, I will obey Your Word and tithe financially, but help me see where I am withholding my tithe of my WHOLE SELF! Jesus gave it all for me, and I want to give my all to You.

Notes

Day 31
The Bread: Silence
James 1:19; Matthew 26:63; Philippians 2:14–15; Luke 23:34; Isaiah 53:7

*D*uring the crucifixion process, Jesus demonstrated a restraint of silence during the difficult times. How often do we complain and murmur, call everyone, tell everyone when we so much as get a hangnail? Never once did Jesus complain, whine, rally the troops, or even get mad and stomp around so everyone could see. Jesus took on the arduous, painful, unjustified attack, beating, horrific abuse, being nailed to the cross, hung to die, and not once did He murmur and complain. Instead, He prayed and asked God to forgive them, for they knew not what they were doing. All we can do is strive to be more like Jesus. Yes, there are times to rally the troops, but NOT to murmur and complain!

Commit as you take this bread to watch your words, behaviors, thoughts, etc., and determine to do what is God's desire. Ask God if you need only to go to Him, or to speak to your leadership, or to others to pray with you. If God directs you to reach out, ask Him with who and what burdens to share. It is crucial to reach out to someone who has the natural and spiritual authority to help, not just those who will commiserate, complain, murmur, and cause strife.

Prayer Starter: Lord, forgive me when I have not gone to You first. When I have murmured, complained, whined, and threw a fit so that everyone's attention could and would be on me and the drama and calamities going on in my life. My first thoughts were not to go to You, Lord. I repent for keeping the focus on me. I ask now, Jesus, for You to teach me to do as You did even in the hardest of times. Help me to seek You first, do as You say, and forgive those who have trespassed against me, even if it was me who trespassed myself. Thank you, Jesus, for being the example for me.

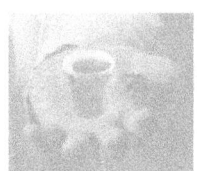

The Cup: Covers Your Sins
Ephesians 4:32; Colossians 3:13; Luke 6:37

*H*ave you ever had those times when you felt what you had done or not done was unforgivable? Or maybe you did not know how you could forgive someone else? It is such a heavy burden. But Jesus carried our burdens on the cross and shed His blood so that WE CAN because He already did it for us.

Regarding ourselves, He forgave us, and when we can't or won't forgive ourselves, we are in a sense telling Jesus all He did to forgive us was useless. Yet, He would do it again if He had to, just for us! So, forgive yourself; He already has.

Regarding others, it hurt Jesus more than us for Him to take on all our hurts, wrongdoings, pain and give us forgiveness forever. When we do not forgive others, we are only hurting ourselves, not them! Yet, Jesus bore that as well. He shed all of His blood to cover us and remove every ounce of our unforgiveness and unbelief of our worthiness to be forgiven.

Accept Jesus' forgiveness as you drink from the cup.

Prayer Starter: Jesus, thank you for going to the cross and shedding all Your blood to forgive me, even those things I believe are unforgivable. You died so that I would be free. You rose so that I would not have to be captive to this world and to the sin and shame that comes with it. You made me worthy to be forgiven and to forgive myself as well as others. I accept Your forgiveness that You have provided me.

Day 32
The Bread: Embrace God's Revelation of the Next Layer of the Onion
Isaiah 53; Mark 10:34; 1 Peter 2:24; Matthew 27:26

*W*hen Jesus was being whipped/scourged[9], and His back was being cut open layer by layer, hit after hit, the pain was excruciating, but it was part of the process, and Jesus took every cut, tear, slicing, and pain for us so we would be healed and covered by the blood that poured out of Him. It is often painful and disturbing each time God reveals to us the next layer of the onion He wants to heal in our life.

Often, we feel cut open, exposed, and vulnerable because we are hurting. It feels unbearable, like all the blood is rushing out of us. We must embrace these times; we have an advocate in Jesus who knows and understands our pain. He does not bring judgment, or condemnation, or shame. He brings His blood to wash us clean, heal us, and He uses these gaping wounds we have tried to hide to infuse His D.N.A. (Divine and Natural Authority) into us. To merge His blood into our wounds and redeem them. Our deepest wounds are what Jesus sacrificed His body for. He counts it all joy to heal us and restore us.

As you take the bread, thank Jesus for sacrificing Himself for you. For taking on the pain and agony so that He could understand and walk you through your pain and misery. Jesus shed His blood to infuse you, heal you, and redeem you!

---

[9] *A Roman judicial penalty consisting of a severe beating with a multi-lashed whip containing embedded pieces of bone and metal.*

Prayer Starter: Oh Jesus, the pain can be unbearable, but You understand far better than anyone else. I feel vulnerable, exposed like everything is seeping out of me, my shame is overwhelming, my guilt intolerable. YOU UNDERSTAND more than anyone, Jesus. Although You were innocent, You took on all of this for me, not only at the cross but as they flogged and tortured You. Jesus, You are my strength, my hope, my savior, my everything. Help me get through the onion layers, through the tears and pain so that I can be more like You.

Notes

Day 32
The Cup: Healing Salve
John 19:34; 1 John 2:1-2; Isaiah 61:1

Oh, the blood of Jesus! What power it holds. It is through our wounds, our cuts, gashes, and brokenness that Jesus infuses the blood He shed when He took it all on Himself at the cross. The blood that flowed during the jabbing of the crown of thorns into his head, to the beatings and whippings, the splinters in His back as He carried the cross (our burdens), and to the nailing of His hands and feet. And with the final blow of the spear piercing the side of Jesus, emptying him of every drop of His blood and water (John 19:34). Jesus did this so His blood, filled with His D.N.A. (Divine and Natural Authority), would have access to us and transform us as we receive the healing only He provides. Then His blood heals the wounds, redeems them, and like Him with His scars, we can advocate for those who need the healing we have received, just as Jesus advocates to our Heavenly Father for us. Thank you, Jesus, for Your blood!

Take the cup in remembrance of the blood of Jesus, which is a healing salve that transforms you, and you will have the opportunity to share the healing power Jesus gives in His blood.

Prayer Starter: Jesus, I can never thank you enough for carrying my burdens on the cross so that I would not have to. It does not take away the emotional and physical pain I am going through, but I know You understand. You had to experience all the emotional and physical pain as well. When you rose from the dead, You demonstrated that I, too, will rise from these difficult times and issues. Just as Your scars were evident, my scars, both the evident and hidden, are being healed. As I heal, I will advocate for You here on Earth as You advocate for me in Heaven.

Notes

Day 33
The Bread: Purposeful
Romans 8:28; Psalm 138:8; 2 Timothy 3:15

Jesus lived, died, and rose with purpose as HIS focus! Every aspect of Jesus' life demonstrates how to live on purpose through our actions, behaviors, thoughts, interactions, and, most importantly, our words. Jesus was not self-focused; His life and ministry were never affected by a pseudo/hypothetical mirror that looked back at Himself. Thus, His focus was always on others and what His Father wanted Him to do. Satan has taught us and sown into us a love for self, more than any other in this world. We speak audibly and inaudibly things Jesus never demonstrated and taught us not to do: assuming everything others do is about us or depending on everyone (including ourselves) to meet our needs when only God can. As well as focusing on what we need and want and leaving the scraps/leftovers for everyone else. Believing lies over the truth of God and living as Me, Myself, and I instead of Father, Son, and Holy Spirit, to name a few. You see, God knew and understood this. He knew we would need a redeemer to come, who dealt with these temptations yet did not succumb to them, so He sent Jesus. Jesus knew He would sacrifice Himself so we could walk in forgiveness and repent and come back to Him and be focused on God.

As you take this bread, focus yourself back on Jesus and not on yourself. Purpose to live your life focused on Jesus, your Savior who walked without fault for you so you can know you are redeemed. You do not have to live Satan's lies that focus you on yourself, leading to destruction.

Prayer Starter: God, help me realize where I am focused on myself and not on You! I had not realized how self-focused I am. In this world, everything is about self. I have areas of my life that I have given myself over to the ways of the world. Teach me, Lord, how to have a God-focus. God-esteem instead of Self-esteem. God-reliance instead of Self-reliance. Help break my ties to self and the ways of this world and learn Your ways.

***To learn more about transitioning from a Self-focus to a God-Focus, be on the lookout for a workbook coming soon on learning how to transition from Self- to God-Focus. ***

Notes

Day 33
The Cup: Blood is a Multi-Faceted Diamond
1 John 1:7, 2:15–17; Matthew 24:24

*O*ften we have been too comfortable with claiming the cubic zirconia stone as a genuine diamond. We accept a fake because it does not cost us so much. And if we lose it—well, oh well. We are so blinded, and in our ignorance, sleep, and bliss, we believe the lie that our cubic zirconia stone is an exquisite diamond. How is this? We have been given the exceedingly most expensive diamond ever cut, and its facets shine in a million directions with the purest of light. You see, Jesus' blood is that diamond, and the Holy Spirit—He is the light. Yet, we have become comfortable with a faulty chip of the cuttings off the main diamond or, even worse, a demonic replica of the real thing that looks beautiful at a slight glance but quickly dulls to black. The real diamond—the blood of Jesus—cuts through the glass and mirrors of our selfishness; it shines in every direction out, not just absorbing the light or blocking it at a surface level. Are we wearing and being the real diamond, or have we been content with the fake counterfeit cubic zirconia? Examine yourself and repent if you have been settling for the counterfeit.

Then, when you drink from the cup, pray that God will remove the old cubic zirconia you have settled for and give you the real diamond—the blood of Jesus. Accept the gift God has for you in Jesus. You will never regret it.

Prayer Starter: Too often in my life, Lord, I have accepted a counterfeit, believing something was better than nothing. Help me see where I have chosen the fake things of this world. Help me know and believe because of the blood of Jesus, I am worthy of the real thing. A diamond with so many facets that You, God, shine in a million directions. I refuse to settle for the counterfeit things of this world any longer.

Notes

Day 34
The Bread: He Did It For All!
Romans 6:23; Matthew 18:30–35; 2 Corinthians 1:30; Colossians 1:13–14

*W*hen Jesus went to the cross, He did it for everyone. There was no clause in what Jesus did. Religion, Satan, and man have written in clauses, limiting the redemption of the finished work of Jesus at the cross. Oh, how Jesus' heart breaks when what He did to save every one of us is withheld from those we do not think "deserve it." Have we become so blinded as well by religion, Satan, self, and judgment that we reserve the redemption of Christ to only those we feel deserve it? Are we the ones breaking God's heart as we let the despised by us go further into darkness and the control of Satan, who is taking so many souls with him because we can't believe God can redeem them? Who in our earthly mind do we unconsciously withhold the redemption of Jesus from? Repent for the condemnation you have believed, renounce the bondage Satan has kept you in, and renounce the service you have been giving to Satan. Ask God to forgive you and change your heart, mind, and ways, and see what He wants you to do. Pray and intercede for the redemption of those people. Take action!

Take this bread as a commitment not to withhold Jesus' redemption from anyone!

Prayer Starter: Forgive me, Lord, for withholding Your redemption from those I have thought were unworthy. Those who I did not tell about You for whatever reason. Lord, You forgave me, redeemed me, and helped me. I do not want ever to withhold what You have done for me from anyone else. Show me, Lord, when I fall into this trap again, and give me the strength to share about Your grace, mercy, and redemption.

The Cup: Power Wash
1 Corinthians 6:11; Psalm 51:2; Ezekiel 37:23

*J*esus' blood does not just cover sin; it has within it the properties that eat up and destroy the destructive, false, evil elements that destroy us and keep us in the world's ways. Jesus's blood heals us, restores us, rewrites our DNA and story, and, most importantly, makes us more like Him. The power of the blood of Jesus has been minimized and stripped of the extensive function it has. It is not just a covering to hide all that makes us unclean. It is the POWER WASH that cleanses us and destroys the antithesis of Christ, and redeems every part of us so that we are infused by the blood of Jesus and restored to holiness. Jesus did not go through all He did to leave us in the brokenness and muck of this world and just throw a cover over us. No! He did it to heal us, infuse us, gird us up, and lift us up so we can walk as He did on the water of His redemptive blood and be a beacon of light to those in the boat being destroyed by this world! Do not take the blood for granted!

Drink and accept the power wash of the blood of Jesus to heal you, infuse you, gird you up, and lift you so you can have all the strength found in the blood. Be a beacon of light to the broken in this world.

Prayer Starter: As you said in Ezekiel, Lord, I make this personal. "I shall not defile myself anymore with my idols and my detestable things or with any of my transgressions. But You will save me from all the backslidings in which I have sinned and will cleanse me; I will be Yours, and You will be my God!" Lord, I commit myself now to the power wash that only the blood of Jesus can do. Heal me, infuse me, gird me up, and lift me up in the strength of the blood of Jesus so I can be the beacon of light to others in this broken world.

Day 35
The Bread: No Other Way!
John 14:6; 1 Timothy 2:5–6a; Romans 8:38–39, 12:1–2

*J*esus said there is **NO OTHER WAY** to the Father but through Him! We are created with the need and desire for connection to our Heavenly Father, who longs for us to be back in communion with Him. Yet, we live in a world controlled by the evil one whose primary focus is to keep us from accepting Jesus, being reconnected with, and communicating with God continually. Think about all the ways we have tried and failed to get the Divine connection, and yet all along, Jesus had paid the price and opened the door for us when He sacrificed Himself for us on the cross. **Jesus is the only way!** What do you need to repent, renounce, and ask for forgiveness for in your life because it has evicted Jesus, thus disconnecting you from the only way to the Father? Once you do that, accept Jesus' forgiveness, ask Him to wash you in His blood as He breaks the bonds and connections to those things and people. Pray that the Holy Spirit fills all those areas and seals you with His power.

Now, continue to do this daily as you take communion. Renew your mind by putting Jesus first and communing with the Father.

Prayer Starter: There are times, Lord, that I feel so far from You. Things in this world have successfully distracted me from the hunger within me to be connected to You. I know You have not left me, Lord; I have disconnected from You. I repent for allowing this world's concerns, wants, desires, needs, **everything** to distract and disconnect me from You, my first love. I renounce the shame, guilt, unforgiveness, offenses, and anything that causes the disconnection, and I ask for Your forgiveness in the name of Jesus. Break all bonds and destructive connections to anything that disconnects me from You. Fill me, Holy Spirit, and seal me with Your Power.

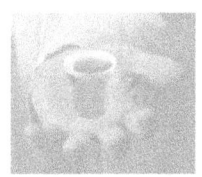

The Cup: Ever-Flowing River
1 John 1:7–9; Hebrews 9:13–14; Colossians 2:13–14; Acts 2:38; Micah 7:19

If we think about a river flowing past us, the molecules passing before us, we will NEVER see it again. This is what our sins are—washed in the blood of Jesus, washed away, never to be seen again by God. Why do we chase down our sins, thinking we must re-live them, then bring them back into everyone's as well as God's remembrance? Jesus' blood is an ever-flowing river that continually washes us clean. When we throw our sins, cares, fears, and brokenness into the river of Jesus' blood, they are washed away. Do not try to go fishing for them. Let Jesus take it away! Right now, think about what you need to repent for and throw in the river; what do you need to stop fishing for, and what joy, praise, and worship you need to give for the beautiful redemption and cleansing by the blood of Jesus.

Take the cup and remember what the blood of Jesus has done for you. Make a promise to God that you will throw into the river those things you have accepted His forgiveness for and that you will not go fishing for them ever again. Take some time to praise and worship God for your freedom.

Prayer Starter: Jesus, thank you for shedding Your blood for me so that my sins that I have repented of are thrown into the ever-flowing river of blood that washes me clean. Forgive me for going fishing for those sins to re-live them, bring them back to my or other's attention or remembrance, and help me, Lord, to not be held captive to what You have washed away. Thank you again, Jesus, for Your redemption and cleansing that allows me to live in Your freedom.

Day 36
The Bread: Missing the Invitation Call!
Luke 14:15-24 (focus on 21-24)

Jesus died and rose for everyone! The Holy Spirit calls from deep within us with an invitation to accept the forgiveness of our sins and eternal life in Heaven with the Lord. We may have grown up in the knowledge of God, or maybe thought we were doing well enough and were automatically invited to Heaven based on our outward activities, that we are a "good person," or based on church attendance and involvement. But when Jesus makes the invitation call for a relationship with Him, we do not hear His call because our lack of intimate relationship with Him hardens our hearts to His call. Our actions say, thanks for all You did, Jesus, BUT I've got more pressing things to do: my nails, work, going out with the guys, or girl's night; the list of excuses is endless! We were not created for this world and our selfish desires. As servants of God, we were sent to Earth with a mission to reach the lost, introduce them to Jesus and make sure they come to the banquet in Heaven. But too often, we become one of the lost as we get embroiled in the cares and pleasures of this world. Then we, too, miss the invitation call and forfeit our invitation. Have you missed the invitation call of Jesus? Repent now, turn back to Jesus, accept the invitation and come feast at Jesus' banquet. The door of opportunity is today! Tomorrow is not guaranteed!

Commit today as you eat this bread. Do not miss your invitation to the banquet table!

Prayer Starter: Oh Lord, I repent right now for the missed invitation calls that You have sent to me because of my focus on other worldly-related things. You have set a banquet table before me, and yet I have chosen the scraps of this world. I make a choice right now to accept the invitation to Your banquet and for eternity with You. Help me to remember I am here for Your purpose, not mine.

Notes

Day 36
The Cup: The Last Gift
Romans 4:7–8; Ephesians 1:7; Matthew 26:28; Hebrews 10:19–20

Jesus shed his blood before, during, and on the cross at Calvary. He emptied himself and died. Jesus then took the keys of eternal death from Satan and rose from the grave, redeemed and filled with the Divine blood of God. Why would He do this? Because God, Jesus, and the Holy Spirit want us, His children, His redeemed, to be saved and blessed. How? The blood of Jesus COVERS our sins, forgives our transgressions, and the Lord only sees the blood of Jesus. So, He will never count our sins and our transgressions against us! What sins or transgressions are you needing to repent and renounce so that you can accept the forgiveness only Jesus can give? He will cover you with His blood, and your unrestricted access will be open to the Lord of lords and Kings of kings.

Take some time to go through this process and ask God to cleanse you of all unrighteousness. Then take this cup as a symbol of the blood of Jesus washing you as white as snow.

Prayer Starter: Jesus, I repent and renounce all of my sins/transgressions, and I am thankful that Your blood COVERS all my sins and forgives me, so when the Lord looks at me, all He sees is Your blood. Thus God will never count my sins or my transgressions against me! Jesus, Your blood covers me and allows me unrestricted access to God, You, and the Holy Spirit.

Notes

Day 37
The Bread: Help to Forgive
Hebrews 7:26; Matthew 6:14–15; Mark 11:25; Luke 17:4; 23:34

Jesus was pure, holy, and blameless, yet he became the sacrifice for us. He was the spotless lamb who had never violated God's ways. Thus, Jesus became our sacrifice so that He could carry every one of our iniquities to the cross for us. He knew our forgiveness by God would require a pure and holy sacrifice. Jesus' sacrifice demonstrates God's love for us. Now because of the shedding of the blood of Jesus resulting in His death, burial, and resurrection, we have the power in the name of Jesus by which we are saved. Jesus is the example of God's heart and desire for forgiveness. We, too, are to walk as Jesus did and have a heart of forgiveness and love for all others in the world. God did not have to forgive us, but because of Jesus' sacrifice - He did! STOP, think, do you have anyone you are justifying your reasons not to forgive? God had millions of reasons, and yet He still forgave.

Examine yourself before you take this bread. Is there anyone you need to seek Jesus' help to forgive? Ask God to faithfully help you through the forgiveness process, revealing the root of the issue.

Prayer Starter: God, You willingly forgave me because of what Jesus did at the cross, being the sacrifice for all my sins, judgments, unforgiveness, everything. You didn't have to, but You did. So, I ask for Your help, Father God, to be as strong as Jesus was and forgive those who have trespassed against me, who have hurt me, and those who I have struggled to forgive. I understand, based on Mark 11:25 that I need to forgive anyone

I'm angry at so that You too can forgive me. Sometimes it feels as difficult as it must have been for Jesus on the cross, but His love demonstrates to me I can do it too.

AFFIRMATIONS

Because of the shedding of the blood of Jesus, resulting in His death, burial, and resurrection, I have the power in the name of Jesus, by which I am saved.

Day 37
The Cup: Blood Replacement
1 Corinthians 5:17; John 14:6; 1 John 3:1–3; Galatians 5:24

Jesus poured all his Divine/natural blood out for us at the cross. When He rose again, He rose with completely Divine blood—no longer mixed with natural/human blood! How do we know this? Because if Jesus had anything less than wholly pure and holy Divine blood, He would never be able to sit next to God. When we come to Jesus, give our life to Him, it is the start of the transition from death to life where our straight human-only blood begins the process of being transfused with the D.N.A. (Divine and Natural Authority) of Christ. During this process, our natural only blood—every cell, molecule, and atom—is being regenerated with Jesus' D.N.A.- it is a process.

This process is helping us to become more and more like Jesus as the D.N.A. in Jesus' blood rewrites our story, and our DNA becomes more powerful, blood flowing in, through, and out of us. We will continually have to die to self (natural/flesh part of us) to become more like Jesus until our final death when all our human/Divine blood is replaced by Divine-only blood, so we too can be in the presence of the Lord in purity.

Take the cup with all the gratitude you have in you for the continual process of blood replacement so you can be more and more like Jesus, and for the future when God determines to fill you with His Divine blood so you can be in His presence in your new body filled with Divine blood only.

Prayer Starter: Jesus, thank you that You are day-by-day, moment-by-moment, changing me from death to life. Your blood that covers me fills me and restores me to who I originally was before coming to Earth. Once here, the focus on self took over, but now that I have given my life back to You, I am in the process of dying to myself so that I can live in You.

Notes

Day 38

The Bread: Not Always Perfect
Philippians 3:13–14; 2 Corinthians 5:17–18

Jesus was perfect, always on time, and did everything God asked Him to do! But God never demands complete perfection from us. Yes, He requires that we endeavor to be in a place of submission to Him, striving to do all He asks of us. But when we miss the mark (sin), as can and will happen, we have Jesus, who died on the cross to cover our imperfections and keep us in right standing with God. Jesus rose from the grave for us, so we know we can walk in the forgiveness He paid in advance. Maybe you have been beating yourself up for not taking communion every day or for maybe even forgetting. The wonderful and amazing part about THIS process is that you can confess, and Jesus forgives you, and you take communion now and keep going with no condemnation!

Thank you, Jesus, for the peace and love You so quickly give us when we come to You.

Prayer Starter: Lord, how often do I judge myself, condemn myself, and feel like a failure because I expect perfection. But this is a lie from the enemy because You do not expect me to be perfect. After all, only Your Son, Jesus, is perfect. Lord, when I miss the mark, when I forget, when I do other things instead of what Your will is, help me not judge myself and instead quickly repent, asking for Your forgiveness and then starting anew. Thank you for Your forgiveness, love, and peace, as well as Your grace, mercy, and righteousness.

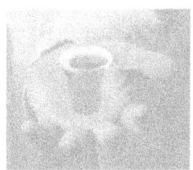

The Cup: Easy to Neglect
John 3:16; Galatians 2:17-21

Oh, how easy it is for us to neglect that we are washed and covered by the blood of Jesus. Just as we may not think about how there is blood pulsing through our veins, how it is all contained within us and pushes around our body with every beat of our heart. We take it for granted until it does not work right or we are cut, and the blood flows out of us or, even worse, stops moving. We do not think about what our blood holds within it, literally the power of life and death. Jesus knew the importance of His blood that it would pay the price for us and heal, restore, redeem and cover us. His blood would ultimately be what allows us access to our Father God. We have been infused with the D.N.A. (Divine and Natural Authority) of Jesus, and His blood flows in, on, and over us in a supernatural way. Do not neglect what we are freely given, yet cost Jesus His life to give. Jesus rose and is at the right hand of God, advocating for us who carry His D.N.A. in our blood. Thank you, Jesus!

Before you take the cup, feel your pulse. Maybe on the inside of your wrist or your neck. Just feel it for a minute, close your eyes, and thank God for your heart that is pumping His D.N.A. from Jesus and your flesh/human blood throughout your body. Also, take a moment to thank Jesus for His heartbeat stopping when He was on the cross so that when yours stops, it will restart in Heaven in your new body with divine-only blood so you can live for eternity in the presence of God. Now, take the cup.

Prayer Starter: Jesus, thank you for going to the cross for me. You shed Your blood and dying so that You could fulfill the promise of death, burial, and resurrection. All so that I can have eternal life just as You do. Just as I have not paid attention to how much my heart and body remain alive because of the human blood flowing through me every second of every day, I have often taken for granted what You did for me, infusing me with Your D.N.A. when I accepted You. Please forgive me, and keep me in remembrance of Your sacrifice for me.

Notes

YOUR GOD-GIVEN DIVINE & NATURAL AUTHORITY

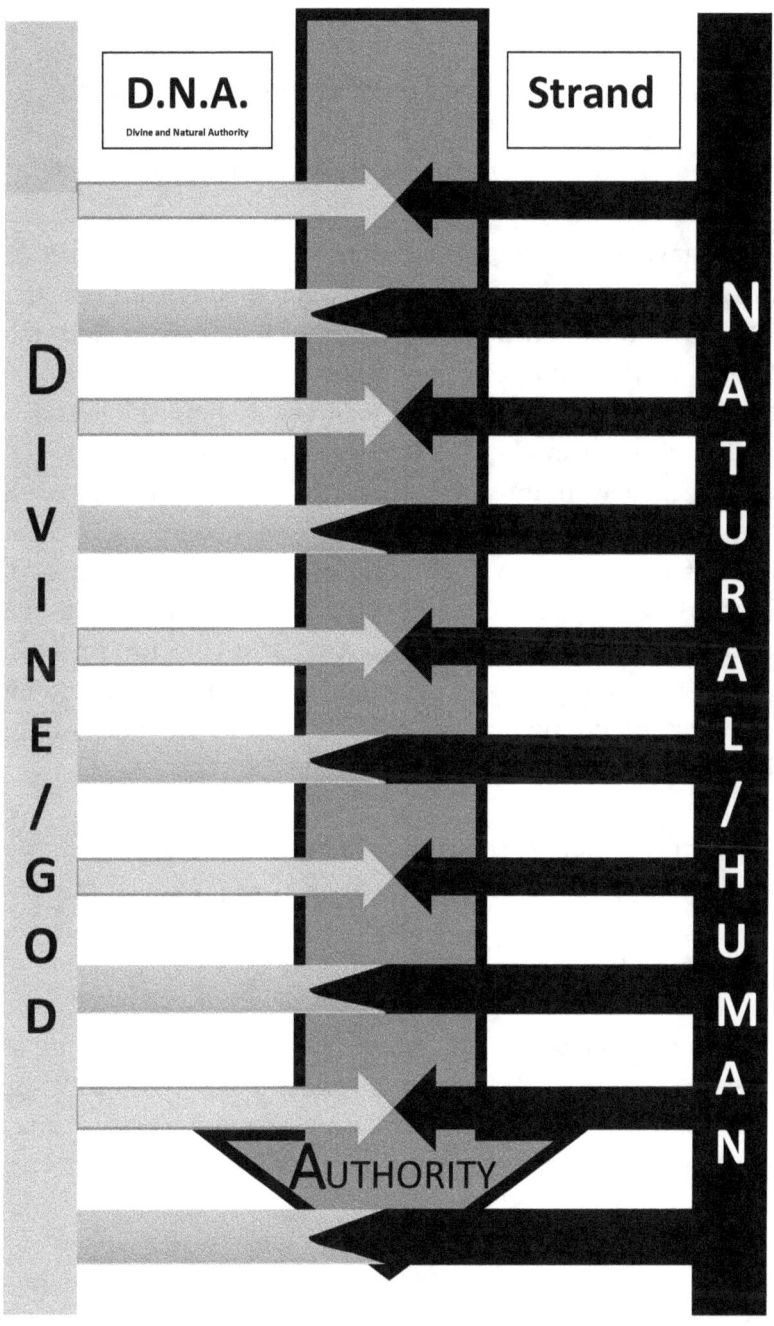

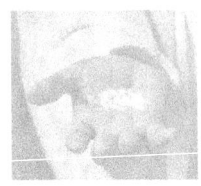

Day 39
The Bread: Determined Focus
Psalm 46:1; Proverbs 3:5-6; Hebrews 4:15-16; Philippians 3:14

*J*esus gave us a clear picture of how to live each day focused on the goals God gave us. When Jesus' mind/body/soul/Spirit and FOCUS were set on the redemption of mankind to God, there was NOTHING that could stop Him. Many things could have stopped Him, derailed Him, or distracted Him; so, He showed us the extremes and how to stay focused and press on. To get to the prize, He went through rejection, pain, abuse, ridicule, being spat on, jeered, beaten, nailed to the cross, not getting to defend himself, remaining silent, betrayal, and so much more. Read the Word/Bible with a focus on the Gospels and look at all Jesus went through to complete the purpose God sent Him for; to redeem us to God through Himself! He had determined focus; nothing would stop Him no matter how big or small, right or wrong; it was not based on others but only God.

Now, take a moment and think about what is distracting you, what is stopping you, what you are allowing to deter or detour you. There is no way they are as severe or barraging as what Jesus went through, and yet He pushed on!

Pray and ask God to reveal what you need to push through and past just as Jesus did. There's no condemnation, instead resolve that you will push on and fulfill your purpose as Jesus did. As you partake of this bread, seek God for the focused determination needed to succeed.

Prayer Starter: Lord, I ask You to forgive me for being distracted, deterred, detoured, or even stopped due to fear, rejection, pain, ridicule, betrayal, and for any other reason. Jesus went through way more than I could ever go through, and yet with Your power and the Holy Spirit, He pressed on toward the mark for the prize of the high calling that You set before Him. Thank you, Lord, that I will never have to go through the levels of difficulty Jesus did. Help me learn to recognize that the determined focus Jesus had now lives in me through Your Holy Spirit. Give me the strength to push on, press forward, and fulfill Your purpose for my life.

Notes

Day 39
The Cup: Bloodshed Must Occur
Luke 15:11–32

*I*n this world, no battle is won without bloodshed. Even Jesus shed His blood to win the battle for our redemption to God. Because of His sacrifice once and for all, we are only required to sacrifice our will to accomplish God's purpose for our existence, which is to bring as many of our brothers and sisters into a relationship with our Heavenly Father. We talk about how we are like the prodigal son coming home to the Father, King of the Heavenly Kingdom, and having all the riches in glory. But the truth is, most of us are more like the prodigal's brother than the prodigal. (Reread the story now focusing on vs. 25-32) We like the brother, angrily say in our hearts, "I have faithfully been serving God, doing everything I am "supposed to do." I obeyed God and did all the "works" a good Christian does"; why hasn't God given me a ministry? And just as the father told the brother, all I have is yours. Sometimes we as believers take our inheritance of the glory, honor, power, and adoration from our Heavenly Father for granted. Our focus is on ourselves, not on the lost! We judge those who were in the world and squandered everything when we were faithful. But God sees the heart of the matter. God is thankful for those who live a "pure and holy" life, and He gladly gives all that is His to those individuals. But like the prodigal's father, our Father is celebratory and happy when His children who were spiritually dead return and are now alive; were lost and have found their way back to Him through the shed blood of Jesus.

Get yourself right with God! Regardless of what brother you have been remembering, Jesus' blood was shed for both of them.

Drink in remembrance of Jesus' blood that is realigning you and preparing you for the celebration God has for you.

Prayer Starter: Lord, if I have been like the prodigal son's brother, forgive me, Father, for my anger, frustration, and irritation that though I lived a "pure and holy life," I do not recognize the blessings that you have given me. Or Lord, if I have been the prodigal son, forgive me and thank you for welcoming me back with open arms, celebrating my return regardless of what I've done. Lord, help me to be understanding toward those who are one or the other of these two. Remind me, Lord, that You sent Your Son Jesus for both the prodigals and the brothers of the prodigals. Help me to not just focus on myself but also long to see those who are lost come back to You.

Notes

Day 40
The Bread: Bodies on the Ground
1 John 1:1–4; John 1:1, 14, 14:12, 26, 16:7;
1 Timothy 2:5; Luke 24:49

God planned for Jesus to be 100 percent human and 100 percent Divine, and 100 percent our Savior so that we could be redeemed back to our Heavenly Father. Jesus would be the only Heavenly Spirit who would walk the earth in human form and be a Divine body (God) on the ground. Jesus was the forerunner and the model of our roles here on Earth. The Word of God says in John 14:12 that we are to do the things Jesus did and even greater things. How? Because Jesus demonstrated it for us, and then when He went back to His Father in Heaven, and God sent us the Holy Spirit (Luke 24:49, John 14:26, and John 16:7). We now have the Lord in the Holy Spirit living in us and giving us all wisdom, power, strength, etc., to do even greater things than Jesus did.

So now, because of Jesus, we are enlisted in the army of God when we accept Him as Lord of our life. We are no longer owned by ourselves or this world. We are a soldier for the Kingdom of God! We are the body on the ground that God needs to subdue, redeem, restore, save, and complete what He must do before He can complete His plan. Commit to take your orders from God, the Commander and Chief, and go to battle with the Lord today!

As you take this bread, thank Jesus for setting a standard and a path for you to be a pivotal part of the process God has planned. You are here today because you are designed for such a time as this.

Prayer Starter: Lord, thank you for giving me Your Holy Spirit who is living in me, filling me with all wisdom, power, strength, etc., to do even greater things than Jesus did! I wholeheartedly embrace my enlistment into Your army. When I accepted Jesus as Lord of my life,

I entered boot camp where I continually learn that I am no longer owned by myself or this world. Instead, I am becoming a soldier for the Kingdom of God! I am one of the bodies on the ground that You, God, made an elite soldier with Christ and the Holy Spirit to complete Your plans and purposes in this world. I commit to taking my orders from You God, the Commander and Chief, and go to battle with and for You today!

Notes

Day 40
The Cup: Written In Blood
1 Corinthians 6:20, 7:23; Galatians 3:13-15; John 3:16; Titus 2:13-14

*J*esus came to earth with the sole purpose to sign the deed for us, this Earth, redemption, the keys to life and death, eternal life in God's Kingdom, healing and deliverance, and to purchase us from the snares of the enemy. But the only way for it to be legal was for Jesus to write it in His blood. He signed the dotted line once and for all in His blood! No higher authority exists! See, Jesus did not just sign with a sprinkle of His blood; NO, He emptied himself completely of His D.N.A. (Divine and Natural Authority) for us and for complete dominion. When we stand before God, He will ask if we, too, signed the contract. The acceptance of Christ as Lord is the only way we sign the contract. Our more profound understanding of who we are, what Jesus did for us, and the ability to fulfill God's will for us only comes as we read and understand the contract (the Word/Bible) signed in Jesus' blood that had already paid the price.

Commit this day to know, read, and understand the contract (the Word/Bible), so you can walk in the fullness of what Jesus signed for with His blood.

Drink the cup as a symbol of signing the contract with Jesus and committing to continue to learn more of what the contract entails.

Prayer Starter: Thank you, Jesus, for signing on the dotted line for me! Help me to understand and do my part of the contract! As I study the Word, reveal to me Holy Spirit all that is included in the signed contract.

Notes

Day 41
The Bread: Humanness
Luke 22:14-20 (focus on verses 14-15)

*J*esus loved His apostles and the human life He had been living after coming from Heaven to Earth to live among His people. Since the beginning of time, Jesus has continually participated with creation but had not had the chance to come to Earth as a human. When the pre-set time had arrived for God to come to Earth in human form, Jesus was then able to experience and understand every aspect of being a natural man. Jesus was able to demonstrate to man God's heart. God's love, compassion, forgiveness, healing, and power is everything God is, was, and will always be. He is the never-changing King of kings! Jesus was so comfortable in His dual citizenship. He enjoyed reclining, relaxing, laughing, and fellowshipping with His disciples, the sick, the children, and all others. However, His disciples/Apostles saddened him the most because they were the closest humans to Him. BUT He knew the hour had come.

As seen in Luke 22:14, Jesus hushed the fun and told them, "**I HAVE EAGERLY** (Jesus looked forward with immeasurable excitement yet sadness) **DESIRED** (this was all part of the plan since before time began) **TO EAT** (to do/partake of the will and plan of God) **THIS** (what He was about to do - Crucifixion/Death/Resurrection) **PASSOVER** (Jesus being the spotless lamb would be the fulfillment of the saving of mankind from the penalty of death due to sin) **WITH YOU** (it would be His last Passover with those closest to him and as a natural man/human) **BEFORE** (before the suffering Jesus would undergo for the redemption of all mankind) **I** (Jesus took it all on Himself) **SUFFER** (not just the cross, but not being human and with us, the suffering of the separation from us would be far worse than the cross).

As you eat this bread, recognize how much Jesus loves you and all He did for you!

Prayer Starter: Jesus, thank you for being willing to come to live among us and die for us, thus giving up the daily intimate interactions with mankind. Oh, the joy and excitement as well as the challenges, frustrations, and pain You experienced living as a human. But You always knew this was not just for fun and enjoyment, but it was to fulfill God's purpose and plan for You to redeem me so that I can spend eternity with Him. Help me recognize my humanness is not what makes me; it's You, Jesus, God, and the Holy Spirit, who makes me who I am called, destined and purposed to be.

Notes

Day 41
The Cup: Enjoying the Time
Luke 22:14-15; Genesis 3:8; 1 John 4:13

Jesus was reclined and relaxed. He was at peace, full of joy and laughter, loving and enjoying the fellowship with His Apostles. Jesus—God Himself who came to Earth in human form to fellowship with His creation again as He did in the Garden of Eden. As Jesus looked around, He knew the time had come. He would once again have to break the physical, human, natural connection—but this time, it was to make a way never to leave His creation again because God's Holy Spirit would fully and completely inhabit those who accepted and believed in Jesus. God created us, and Jesus became like us and took on flesh and blood, knowing that had to be so we would honestly know God and intimately understand Him. Jesus knew that He would have to suffer the loss of His flesh and blood to leave us the Spirit of God. Why? Because only then could Jesus show us that if we accept Him and all He did while living as we do, following in His footsteps and putting our flesh to death, we too could live in the Divine as He did and does now and for eternity.

How loving and good is God that not wanting to be separated from us; He sent His Holy Spirit to remain with us until we are once again in His presence. God's Holy Spirit came to Earth to be in us and for the fulfillment of His divine plan. Now we have all power in our DNA through the blood of Jesus and God's Holy Spirit within us.

Drink from this cup in remembrance of the immeasurable pleasure Jesus had in being with God's created beings. Jesus sacrificed His temporary time here on Earth by going to the cross so that He could make a way to be with us for eternity.

Prayer Starter: Jesus, I can only imagine as You sat at the table looking at Your Apostles, how much You enjoyed being with them and interacting with all God's creation. To look at them and know that by going to the cross, dying for them, You would be assuring their ability to spend eternity with You. Jesus, I don't take for granted what You did for me. Thank You for loving me so much that You became my sacrifice so that I can know You, God, and now be filled with God's Holy Spirit. God, thank you for loving me so much that You sent the full measure of Your Holy Spirit to live in me so that I am Divinely connected to you.

Notes

Day 42
The Bread: Last Meal
Luke 22:16; Hebrews 9:22–28; 1 Corinthians 5:7; Psalm 103:12

*J*esus told the apostles why he had eagerly desired to eat the Passover meal with them in verse 16. Read it! What was Jesus meaning? He says, "**FOR I** (Jesus) **TELL YOU** (believers). **I WILL NOT EAT** (partake, experience, enjoy, indulge, or saver) **IT** (the meal that represented Him: See Hebrews 9:22–28; it is also Jesus' humanness. He would soon be sacrificing Himself, and the human side of Him would die) **AGAIN** (once and for all) **UNTIL IT FINDS** (when Jesus comes to rapture us) **FULFILLMENT** (completeness of God's plan) **IN THE KINGDOM OF GOD** (not in the earthly kingdom of Satan). Jesus knew this would be His last Passover meal. He was to become the fulfillment of what it symbolized. We now celebrate what Jesus did when He died once and for all for us—redeeming us and washing away our sins when we repent. He sends them as far as the east is from the west (Psalm 103:12). Jesus chose to die for our sake and will not return until we return with Him in our supernatural bodies to rule and reign with God.

Eat this bread, thank Jesus for all He did, and for showing how you must die to your flesh and humanness to live like Him.

Prayer Starter: Jesus, when You died on the cross, You demonstrated how important it is that I place my flesh on the cross as well. This is the only way to follow You wholly and completely. Thank You for sacrificing Your body so that even when I fail in the process of dying to my flesh, You cover me and help me walk within and yet through my humanness to be more like You.

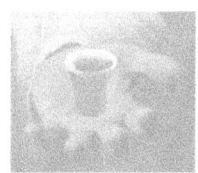

The Cup: Share
Luke 22:17; Hebrews 10:19;
Romans 5:6–11; Ephesians 1:3–14

Jesus took the cup holding the wine that represented His blood. The blood that redeems heals and restores us. Jesus blessed and gave thanks to God, knowing He would shed every ounce of His D.N.A. (Divine and Natural Authority) in His blood at the cross. God's plan was Jesus' blood would be the last sacrifice ever required for the forgiveness of sins and would be the entryway into the Holy of Holies for our communion with God Himself. Jesus' blood would allow God's Holy Spirit to reside in us, work through us, and be one with us. Jesus commanded, "**TAKE THIS** (the blood of Jesus and everything His blood gives us) **AND DIVIDE IT** (share it, give it, <u>do not</u> hoard it to ourselves only but continually give it away) **AMONG YOU.** (Not for us alone, but for EVERYONE!)

Prayer Starter: Jesus, I thank you that You loved me so much that You died for me. I take this cup in remembrance of the blood You shed to redeem, heal and restore me. It removes from me the evil strongholds of this world and is the power given to me by the Holy Spirit, allowing me to boldly come into the Holy of Holies to have my own special communion with God. I can live boldly because of God's Holy Spirit living in me. Help me to share what You've done for me with others so that they too can experience this communion.

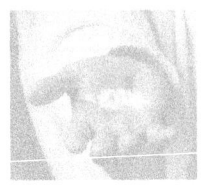

Day 43
The Bread: Chose to Die!
Luke 22:19; John 6:33, 35, 48, 51

*J*esus knew the time had come when His body would be sacrificed for the redemption of God's chosen! Four times in the Book of John (6:33, 35, 48, 51), Jesus tells us He is the Bread of Life. In verse 51, Jesus said, "This bread is my flesh to give life to the world." In Luke 22:19, **JESUS TOOK BREAD** (His flesh), **GAVE THANKS** (to God for what the sacrifice of His body would provide for us) **AND BROKE** (breaking the ties to His flesh, this world, and to the closeness He had with the people) **IT** (His body) **AND GAVE IT TO THEM** (to all of them despite knowing they would betray Him, even Judas who betrayed Jesus for money and Peter who denied Him three times), saying "**THIS** (bread) **IS** (not a counterfeit) **MY BODY** (His flesh, human side) **GIVEN** (not forcefully taken, but a choice made by Jesus to give) **FOR YOU** (everyone); **DO THIS** (eat the bread [of life] daily—any and every time we can) **IN REMEMBRANCE** (never forget Jesus chose to die for us so we can have redemption, eternal life, and an open door to connect personally with the Godhead) **OF ME** (Jesus, the Savior of the world).

Take this bread and remember, Jesus died for everyone—no limit to whom—so you are redeemed and one with God through Him.

Prayer Starter: Jesus, thank you for being the Bread of Life. I know You willingly chose to die so that I can have redemption and eternal life, communion and opened the door to connect personally with God, You, and the Holy Spirit.

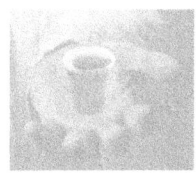

The Cup: Jesus Died to His Humanness so Your Humanity Would Not Be the Death of You
Luke 22:18; 1 Corinthians 15

Jesus promised us that until He comes again, He will only live as a Divine being. When the Kingdom of God comes again, Jesus will return to take us to Heaven.

In Luke, Jesus says, "**FOR I** (Jesus) **TELL** (promise, explain, make clear) **YOU** (all of us) **I WILL NOT** (never again) **DRINK** (partake of) **AGAIN** (since He was conceived) **FROM** (anything in this world) **THE FRUIT OF THE VINE** (wine) **UNTIL** (from then till a future time) **THE KINGDOM OF GOD COMES** (after all believers are resurrected to Heaven, then the battle, and during the millennial reign).

Jesus chose to leave us and not be "human" so He could return to God and sit in the place of authority as God's right-hand powerhouse and advocate for us.

While here on Earth, we remain in our human bodies that carry the Holy Spirit. However, in this world, there is trouble (the enemy), which results in wounds and scars we carry. Through the blood of Jesus, we are healed from this world's damage. Jesus was broken for our brokenness and rose so we can rise from anything that has held us captive. Jesus, as our advocate, understands our hurts, burdens, brokenness and covers us when we go to Him, making a way for us to be redeemed to God.

Thank Jesus for His sacrifice as you drink the cup.

Prayer Starter: Jesus, thank you for dying to Your human flesh and being raised with an incorruptible, immortal body just as we will when You return for us. But, in the meantime, You are advocating for me to God, covering me with Your blood so that no matter what this world does to me or what I do in this world and no matter the battles fought with the powers of this world, You redeem and put me in right standing with God. Help me see that You cover in Your love, forgiveness, and holiness all things that would hinder me from walking righteously.

Notes

Notes

Day 44
The Bread: Living Sacrifice
Romans 8:29, 12:1

*J*esus was our living sacrifice. He knew the importance of the role God had given Him. He knew His sacrifice would then pass the baton to the Holy Spirit.

How are we a living sacrifice? Are we meandering through life, or are we committing ourselves to sacrifice all God asks of us while we are still living and being in this world? Take some time today to evaluate and see if there is anything God would desire for you to pour out as a sacrifice that is pleasing to Him.

Take time to ask and hear from God through His Holy Spirit living in you….listen for that still small voice prompting you to make a sacrifice so that you too can fulfill the role God has had for you since before time (Romans 8:29).

As you eat the bread, ask God to help you through the process of sacrificing those things. He will be with you and help you because He loves you and wants you to be all He created you to be.

Prayer Starter: Jesus, You sacrificed yourself for me, and now I choose to be a living sacrifice for You. Help me in the process of giving back to You everything that You have given me: my life, my hopes, plans, and desires, as well as my time and money. Help me see and understand the benefits of my sacrifice. With the help of Your Holy Spirit, I choose to be a living sacrifice every day of my life.

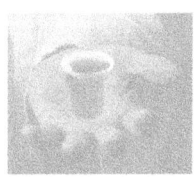

The Cup: New Covenant
Luke 22:20 (EXB); Romans 3:25-26

*a*ll things are significant. At the beginning of the meal, Jesus broke the bread, symbolizing His body and how He had first come to be with them. However, He waited until after supper to take the cup(v. 20), symbolizing the finality of the cross and Jesus' blood being poured out for our redemption. Jesus wants us to remember that the cup represented the NEW COVENANT IN His blood! What is the new covenant? That once and for all Jesus, the Spotless Lamb of God, would sacrifice Himself, and His blood was the final blood to be shed for our forgiveness. His sacrifice would open the door of communion with God and the Holy Spirit. Jesus' blood held our new/authentic D.N.A. (Divine and Natural Authority), and every drop of it was poured out for us for all eternity!

Drink from this cup as a commitment to live in the New Covenant that Jesus provided for you.

Prayer Starter: Thank you, Jesus, for fulfilling the sacrifice for my past, present, and future sin so I can walk with God and fulfill His purpose in my life!

Day 45
The Bread: No More Shackles, No More Chains!
Luke 22:1–6

*W*hen Jesus went to the cross, He was nailed through His wrists to the cross; it was like being handcuffed, held down, unable to do anything like extending His hands in healing, to hug, and to touch. Then they crossed His feet and nailed them to the cross, shackling His feet from freely moving. Jesus showed us how the world and "religion" will bind us and try to shackle and cuff us to their ways. They will try to nail us down to their rules and regulations that only honor the evil one, Satan. But Jesus took that on for us to have complete freedom. See, Jesus died on a man-made cross that the religious elite determined was fit for this blasphemous man, thus showing us that "religion" without a relationship IS death. But once removed from the world's ways and the hand of "religion" and placed in the grave—Jesus rose victorious! There are songs we sing stating no more shackles, no more chains celebrating our freedom in Jesus. His victory provides us with the ability to live free, not bound to this world or "religion," but in a relationship with Him.

Prayer Starter: Jesus, when You went to the cross, not only did You do it to save me, but You did it to show me the effect of "religion" without a relationship; how it will handcuff me and shackle me, not allowing me the opportunity to do what You created me to do. I thank You that You have broken off the chains and shackles holding me down to the ways of this world and the bondage of religious ways. So now just as You rose from the grave, I rise from that bondage; victorious and free to do Your will.

Freedom
By Matthew Bushard
Adapted by Eddie James[10]

I wanna clap a little louder than before
I wanna sing a little louder than before
I wanna jump higher than before
I wanna shout louder than before

Freedom x8

I wanna clap a little louder than before
I wanna sing a little louder than before
I wanna spin wilder than before
I wanna shout louder than before

Freedom x8

I wanna lift my hands higher than before
I wanna love you more than before
I wanna worship deeper than before
I gotta scream louder than before

Freedom x8

No more shackles
No more chains
No more bondage
I am free

Hallelujah x11

---

[10] *https://www.youtube.com/watch?v=YnOkOp5qQw8*

Day 45
The Cup: Determination
Isaiah 50:7; Philippians 3:12-14, 4:13; Acts 20:24

*W*hat Jesus accomplished at the cross was done by the determination that exuded throughout every aspect of Jesus. It started when God determined before creation that Jesus would be our Savior and how Jesus would be symbolically woven throughout the Old Testament. God had a plan for when Jesus would come to Earth through Mary and under what circumstances. From conception, determination was woven into Jesus' D.N.A. (Divine and Natural Authority). Jesus was determined to (even as a man) obey and do the will of His Father. He was determined to heal, reveal, and restore mankind; He was determined to fulfill His purpose on Earth as determined by God. Jesus went to the Garden of Gethsemane to receive the resolve and the determination to endure the cross boldly. The determination He came out with during this time with God endowed Him with the determination to persevere. With determination, He died, took from Satan the keys to death and the grave, and then resurrected victoriously—all for our sake!

Take this cup to remember Jesus' determination and pray to live with that level of determination every moment of your life. It is only with the blood of Jesus and with the power of the Holy Spirit that you can, and will, live with the same level of determination.

Prayer Starter: Lord, I set within me an ever-growing desire to do Your will and not mine. Give me the determination Lord that You have, Jesus has, and the Holy Spirit has. I want and commit to live in a higher level of determination. Thank you, Lord.

Notes

Day 46
The Bread: Once Bitten, Twice Shy! Stretch!
Matthew 12:11–13; John 21:16; Hebrews 13:20–21

𝓕or many of us, maybe even you, deep inside, we feel we have a lifetime of disappointments, failures, shame, guilt, rejection, abandonment, anger, etc. We hide it like the shriveled hand—constantly reminding us, crippling us, and hindering us from moving forward in life. But Jesus! Even in this passage in Matthew 12:11–13, Jesus expounds on the sheep being saved by the shepherd if it falls into a pit (of despair). We, as people, are even more valuable. (It's interesting to note that Jesus is the Great Shepherd, and we are His sheep [John 21:16, Hebrews 13:20–21]). In Matthew 12:13, Jesus says to us; <u>Stretch out your hand</u> (try again, reach out to Jesus, trust and believe in Him to take all that your 'shriveled hand' represents in you, and heal it. He died to take it all on Himself). When we do, Jesus will restore us to brand new, removing all that held us captive; it will be removed when we reach out to Jesus. Obey His command to stretch out your hand and watch what Jesus will do—regardless of the opinions of anyone else!

Take this bread as an act of stretching out your hand today.

Prayer Starter: Jesus, my lifetime of disappointments, failures, shame, guilt, rejection, abandonment, and anger have held me captive, causing me to shrivel up, thinking and believing I'm unworthy. But today, I hear You calling for me to give You a chance and to stretch out my hand so that You can heal me. I don't care what anyone else thinks; I need You, Jesus. I need You to restore my shriveled heart to a whole and complete heart that only You can give me.

The Cup: Many Will Not Believe!
Mark 16:12-13; Hebrews 13:2; Isaiah 1:18

*H*ave you walked through your life just as these two people/disciples of Jesus walked in the country when Jesus appeared to them? Jesus showed Himself to them, but He did not look the same as before. So many times in our lives, we are going through life, and suddenly, Jesus shows up. As the Scripture in Hebrews says, "welcome strangers, we may be entertaining angels."

That encounter changes us, and we want to tell everyone; however, no one wants to believe. We know we are transformed, changed as Jesus reveals to us that He died for us, for our sins, for all that has, is, and will occur in our life journey, and, most importantly, He rose from the dead, is alive, and will forever be our Savior! We accept this realization and know it is true—Jesus is alive and has come and met with us. We tell everyone and even try to demonstrate a redeemed lifestyle, but do not be surprised, upset, or hurt when others do not believe us, just as no one believed these two men.

Do not let it affect what you know; you met Jesus, and His blood washed you white as snow (Isaiah 1:18). And He continually meets you in your life and is transforming you and proving over and over His great love for you. Do not be moved by others' unbelief!

Drink from this cup in remembrance of how Jesus meets YOU right where you are and walks with YOU, transforming YOU. It does not matter what anyone else thinks or believes because YOU know Jesus met with YOU and washed YOU white as snow!

THE D.N.A. OF COMMUNION

Prayer Starter: Jesus, thank you for meeting me right where I was in my brokenness and sin. I know You have transformed me and that I am no longer the person I used to be.

Lord, I have found myself hurt and upset when others would not see or acknowledge the changes You have made in me. Help me to realize what You did was for me, not for them. Their unbelief does not deter me from knowing You have washed me as white as snow.

Notes

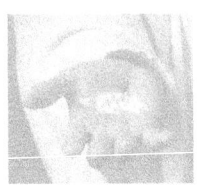

Day 47
The Bread: Old Ways
Colossians 3:1-17; Romans 8:6; Jeremiah 17:9; Proverbs 3:5-6; Philippians 4:6-7

*W*hat if Jesus had only listened to his human side when it came time for Him to go to the cross for us? Would He have completed the purpose God planned for Him? Jesus gave us the demonstration of how to fulfill God's purpose for us. As humans, we are moved, motivated, and conformed by our emotions, feelings, desires, wants, and whims. We tend to make our decisions based on our limited, selfish, self-centered understanding and focus. Our "feelings" drive our lives in every way. Yet, Satan most often is the one driving our emotions, feelings, patterns, hurts, and decisions unless we make the conscious choice to turn it all over to Jesus. Then the Holy Spirit guides us, drives us, and teaches us how to do what God desires for us. What God is feeling, thinking, wanting, desiring instead of our human/evil ways, desires, feelings, wants, etc. Pay attention to your words and thoughts; be very attentive to when there are more "I feel" thoughts or statements than "Lord, what do You think, feel, want, need, etc." This is an excellent way to tell when we have fallen back into our human ways. Ask for forgiveness, and God will help us get back on track. The Holy Spirit will teach us how to do God's will, not our will.

Before you take this bread, ask the Holy Spirit to remove the scales from your eyes regarding where you are being moved more by the concerns of this world than the concerns of God's world.

Prayer Starter: Lord, help me recognize when the enemy is controlling my feelings, emotions, and desires. His goal is to kill, steal, and destroy me. Help me to recognize how much I base my life on my feelings instead of You. Holy Spirit, teach me how to focus on and do God's will, not this world's will. I ask You to remove the scales from my eyes to see and know that You, God, are good and that Your plans for me are good.

Notes

Day 47
The Cup: Conscious Effort
Galatians 5:24; Colossians 3:5; Romans 6

Jesus shed his blood at the cross for us. Jesus demonstrated throughout His life that His D.N.A. (Divine and Natural Authority) existed within Him, so He had to make the conscious effort to decide which part of Him would move and motivate Him. When He died and shed all His blood for us, it was a demonstration of putting the human side to death for the glory of the Divine. We were given the Divine blood to cover us, merge into our humanness, and rewrite our DNA with the "D"ivine in first place. Our "N"atural, human, earthly, part of us that is subject to evil-driven ways, authority, desires, and power MUST take second place to the "D"ivine authority which reigns supreme.

Even Jesus went to God in the garden and asked for another way, but his "N"atural flesh asked. However, Jesus yielded to the "D"ivine and walked in "D"ivine authority while His "N"atural flesh had to bow and take on the pain, agony, cuts, bruises, and destruction so that God's plan would be completed. Jesus lined up to God and was able to complete His mission even in the harshest of conditions. Easy, NO, but worth it!

When you drink from this cup, ask the Holy Spirit to guide you to do as Jesus did and learn how to put your "N"atural human side to death so that the "N"atural authority will take its rightful place <u>behind</u> the "D"ivine authority in you.

Prayer Starter: Holy Spirit, I ask You to guide me to do as Jesus did and put my "N"atural human side to death so that the "D"ivine authority that Jesus gave me at the cross will take its rightful place in me. Help me recognize when my "N"atural flesh opposes my "D"ivine authority. No matter what comes my way in this life, I will stand firm with "D"ivine authority as Jesus did when He took on the cross.

Notes

Day 48
The Bread: Sustenance
Hebrews 4:16, 9:11–22, 10:10; John 14:16–17, 25–26

*W*ebster's dictionary defines sustenance as a means of support, maintenance, or subsistence (living); food (nourishment) provisions; the act of sustaining, the state of being sustained; a supply or being supplied with the necessaries of life; and something that gives support, endurance, or strength.[11]

Wow, re-read those definitions with the understanding that taking this bread is in remembrance of how Jesus sacrificed Himself as the unblemished Lamb so we wouldn't have to sacrifice a lamb again for our sins/missed marks. Jesus redeemed us once and for all. Jesus made it possible to go humbly before the throne of grace, repent, and receive forgiveness and righteousness. Jesus embodies this whole definition as our sustaining source of true Kingdom living, true love, and as all we need. Still, Jesus did not stop at redeeming us—God sent His own Holy Spirit to support us, give us endurance to the end, and the strength to do all God needs us to do.

Eat this bread with thankfulness that Jesus is your complete sustenance. He provided you with all you will ever need to complete your purpose. Go now to the source as you take and eat His body that sustains you.

Prayer Starter: Jesus, You are my sustenance, support, maintenance, and subsistence (living). You provided me with Your Word, ways, and wonders as food (nourishment)

---

[11] *Merriam-Webster. (n.d.). Sustenance. In Merriam-Webster.com dictionary. Retrieved June 22, 2020, https://www.merriam-webster.com/dictionary/sustenance*

provisions. You, Jesus, sustain me with Your Holy Spirit. You have supplied me with all the necessaries of life, and You sent Your Holy Spirit to support me and give me endurance and strength to fulfill my purpose here on Earth.

Notes

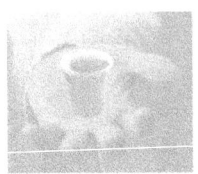

Day 48
The Cup: Wound Care!
Psalm 46:1, 147:3; Hebrews 9:14; 1 John 1:7–9

*G*od is our refuge and strength, an ever-present help in trouble! Blood is known to have all we need to sustain life, heal us, and transport all that is needed within the body from one place to the other. Jesus shed all His blood to cover, redeem, heal, and save us. When we cut ourselves, what happens? We bleed. This process cleanses the wound, and the white blood cells and all the other clotting and healing elements rush to that area to stop the bleeding and heal the body. So too with the blood of Jesus when we accept Him as our Lord and Savior.

As you take the cup, envision the blood of Jesus pouring into your wounds, bringing the healing only Jesus can do. Allow the Holy Spirit to show you even the wounds you have covered up that poison you. Allow the Holy Spirit to gently remove the cover, wash and clean the wound, and then allow Jesus' blood to cleanse and heal the wound. Yes, this is a process, but today is the starting point of complete healing!

Prayer Starter: Thank you, Jesus, for shedding Your blood so that my internal brokenness and wounds I have hidden and are killing me from the inside out will be healed by Your blood. When I come to You, repent, seek You, and open myself to Your healing touch, You are faithful to heal me from the inside out. Thank you, Jesus, for the healing Your blood provides!

Notes

Day 49
The Bread: Take Up Your Cross!
Luke 9:23; 2 Corinthians 10:4; Ephesians 4:9–10

*W*hen times got tough, Jesus never gave up! While in the garden, He sweated blood as He prayed for God to find another way. He knew what torture was to come. Even Jesus had to set His mind not to quit no matter what. It was God's will, not His, that was to be done. He took it all! He carried the heavy cross on His ripped-to-shreds back over a bumpy road as far as He could until He needed help, and one from the crowd carried it. He willingly laid down His life. When He said, "It is finished," His flesh died, His spirit went to the grave where Jesus took all Satan's power and the keys to death and the grave (Psalm 49:15, 86:13, 89:48; Revelation 1:8; Acts 2:31; 1 Corinthians 15:26). Then, in three days, He rose victorious (how often do we give up when the 'death' and resurrection is not immediate?)

In our life, how quickly do we give up? Think about it; if we were in Jesus' place, would we have the tenacity of Jesus? Thank God most of us, at least here in America, will hopefully never have to find out in that literal sense. However, it is easy to throw up our hands under even the slightest challenge, difficulty, or when we are hurt, disappointed, delayed, or when we trust our feelings and believe the lie that God is distant and does not care, etc. When the bumps in the road dig deeper into our wounded self, do we reach out for help from God/Jesus/Holy Spirit or believe we do not have anyone to reach out to. How often does reaching out to God not even cross our minds? Here in Luke 9:23, Jesus says, "To follow Him, you must deny yourself, take up your cross daily and follow Him." When those difficult times come, we must say, "it is done." We are done and must die to our flesh and follow the leading of the Holy Spirit. Let the Holy Spirit deal with the battle; then obey and rise as a new creature in Christ.

Prayer Starter: Jesus, thank you for never giving up, for not quitting when you experienced the torture of the cross. Thank you for demonstrating a tenacity that shows me I have the capacity to stand and to trust that You have already fought the battle and won. Help me realize that You, God, and the Holy Spirit are in me, so when the difficult times come, I have the strength to stand knowing You have already gotten the victory for me.

Notes

Day 49
The Cup: Time to Drink!
John 4:14[12], 18:11; Luke 21:34–36, 22:20; Matthew 20:22, 26:39; 1 Corinthians 11:25–2

*B*efore Christ's crucifixion, when Jesus spoke of drinking, it was often in reference to taking part in the most painful and challenging experience He would ever go through (Matthew 20:22, 26:39; John 18:11). At the last supper, though, Jesus tells us to drink from the cup of the new covenant. The shedding of His blood for our redemption and salvation is what it stood for (1 Corinthians 11:25–26, Luke 22:20). He would go to the cross and shed every milliliter of Himself for us. Then after He rose from the grave, He used "drink" for us to drink in the water of the Holy Spirit—God Himself who lives in each of us by His Holy Spirit (John 4:14 The Passion Translation [see footnote from Gateway.com]).

We are not to drink in the cares of this world but drink in the redemption, salvation, healing, restoration, and all that Jesus was, is, and will be. We are to partake of all Jesus died to give us! Drink in His goodness, mercy, grace, forgiveness, love, compassion, courage, and an unending supply of so much more.

---

[12] *John 4:14, The Passion Translation: "but if anyone drinks the living water I give them, they will never be thirsty again. For when you drink the water I give you, it becomes a gushing fountain of the Holy Spirit, flooding you with endless life!" The Greek verb for "springing up" is hallomenou, and is never used for inanimate objects (water). It is a verb used for people (living things), and means "jumping" or "leaping up." The Septuagint translates this verb elsewhere as an activity of the Holy Spirit.*
https://www.biblegateway.com/passage/?search=John+4%3A13-15&version=TPT

As you prepare yourself to drink the cup, meditate on what it means to you to drink in the redemption, salvation, healing, restoration, and all that Jesus was, is, and will be.

Prayer Starter: Lord, as I drink this cup, I drink in Jesus' goodness, mercy, grace, forgiveness, love, compassion, courage, and an unending supply of so much more. I refuse to drink in the cares of this world, but instead, to drink in all, You have provided for me. I drink in the full power and manifestation of the Holy Spirit, in and through me.

Day 50
The Bread: Die To Self
Colossians 3:1–17; Ephesians 4:22–24; Proverbs 3:5–6; Romans 8:13; Galatians 2:20

Communion is done to remember what Jesus went through physically and, ultimately, died, so we can see we must die to this world with its evil, destroying, hurtful ways. Even if we lived in the world and indulged lavishly in all the worldly desires, WHEN we accept Jesus and all He did at the cross for us, we decide to put to death (daily, hourly, minute-by-minute) our flesh, our old sinful ways. Our commitment was to turn from our previous ways and continually pursue to learn Jesus' ways to become more and more like Jesus, who is God Himself in human form. And we do not have to do it alone—Jesus advocates for us to our Father God, who sits in the mercy and grace seat. When Jesus left Earth and returned to Heaven, God sent the Holy Spirit to live in and through us. So, daily, we have continual opportunities to practice laying our life down as Jesus did and dying to our flesh.

Meditate on how you can focus on Jesus and die to yourself a little more today. Allow the Holy Spirit to guide you through this process moment by moment.

Prayer Starter: Thank you, Jesus, for all You did for me. You filled me with the Holy Spirit so I can live and walk as You did! I do not have to do this life alone; You have provided a way for me to be guided continuously. Help me, Holy Spirit, to see where I need to lay down my life, desires, and ways so that I can be more like Jesus.

The Cup: It Is Available To You!
Romans 2:4, 6:11, 14, 9:14–18; Ephesians 1:4–6, 2:8–9, 4:22–24; Matthew 22:14

God stated that He has mercy on those He has mercy for and compassion for those He has compassion for; thus, it does not depend on our human desires or effort. It depends on God's mercy; once we die to self and rise with Christ (Romans 6:11), we put away our old ways and pursue Christ (Ephesians 4:22–24). But even getting to that point is by God's mercy, compassion, and grace calling us to repentance. As we take this cup, remember that God already sent His only Son to die for us, so God's grace, mercy, and compassion are already available to us. Why? Because God raised us for this very purpose that He might be glorified and display His power in and through us, and so His name would be declared/proclaimed in all the earth. Every drop of blood Jesus shed was blood to cover us—to mark us as one chosen by God, loved and filled with eternal purpose.

Prayer Starter: Thank you, God, for choosing me, even from before time, then sending Your Son to die for me so that I can live in Your grace, mercy, and compassion. Help me get a clearer understanding of the purpose You have for me so that You will be glorified and Your power will be declared and proclaimed in all the earth through me.

Day 51
The Bread: Turn Back To Jesus!
Zechariah 1:3; Jeremiah 24:7; Deuteronomy 4:30; Luke 15:11–32

*A*fter Jesus died on the cross, all who had walked close to Him, talked with Him, heard Him teach, and learned from Him were undoubtedly devastated, unable to understand how this could happen. It was the jumble of emotions we all go through in the grief process when we lose a loved one, especially when it is sudden, unexpected, or horrific. Three days went by—three agonizing days. Oh, the distance they must have felt. Being disconnected, numb, and then having to be obedient to the "sabbath" rules and regulations. Have you found yourself there? You know God is alive, you have an intimate, connected relationship, spend lots of time talking to the Holy Spirit, learning from Him through the Word—and then life happens. Maybe it is a slow creep-in, or maybe a sudden crash and burn! We get hurt, or some other situation or emotions derail us. However, it happens, fast or slow, we begin to realize the distance is vast from where we were with God to where we are now. Trust and know God did not go anywhere—we did! Well, today, come back, determined to return to the closeness again. God is there; run toward Him. He is waiting for us with open arms. Just as the disciples embraced Jesus, fellowshipped with Jesus, and then carried the message of Jesus. God is not dead, nor is our relationship with Him!

Take and eat the bread, feeling it enter inside of you, symbolizing how close God truly is; His Holy Spirit is IN you, thanks to Jesus' death, burial, and resurrection!

Prayer Starter: Thank you, Lord, for NEVER LEAVING ME NOR FORSAKING ME!!!! Even if I get overwhelmed by life and "forget" You. Help me, Jesus, not to believe the lie that it has just been too long. Because I know You are right there waiting for me to return to You and put You first in my life.

Notes

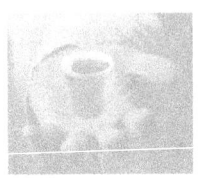

Day 51
The Cup: Get Refilled!
John 19:34–37; Matthew 27:57–61;
1 Corinthians 15:35–57; Romans 5:9

*W*hen Jesus died on the cross, and the soldier pierced His side, and blood and water poured out—Jesus was emptied of **ALL** His blood—lifeless He was laid in the tomb. But when He rose, God had filled Him with Divine blood, a blood that has forever covered us and our sin so God can look at us and see purity, holiness, His unblemished children. But we often forget this—things happen in our lives—good things, bad things; we are caught up in the mundane, drug around by the "life" we live daily. Being run by the needs and wants of everyone else, we begin to realize the emptiness inside, a feeling of distance from our first love. We realize we can't remember the last time we met with God and talked with Him; looking for our Bible, we find it under a pile of stuff; looking in our journal, we realize it's been weeks or months since we wrote while we spent time with God.

Do not stay in that place of emptiness; even Jesus was empty for three days. But God filled Him again. Jesus died for you, so you can always return to Him and be refilled and reconnected.

Sit and enjoy the Holy Spirit, the river of God refreshing you as you reconnect through the blood of Jesus to the one and only Living GOD. When you are ready, take and drink the cup symbolizing the washing of the blood of Jesus.

Prayer Starter: Lord, I feel dead, empty, alone. I let life get in the way of my relationship with You. Forgive me! Lord, help me open the spigot of Your free-flowing Holy Spirit by reconnecting with You. Thank you that I can instantly feel You flowing within me as soon as I reconnect to You!

Notes

Day 52
The Bread: Daily Bread!
John 6:47–58; Matthew 4:4; Deuteronomy 8:3; Matthew 6:11

In John 6:47–58, Jesus stated that He is the Bread from Heaven—the bread of life. He says in verse 51 that the bread is His flesh. Then in verses 53 through 58, He speaks of eating His flesh (bread) and drinking His blood (juice), symbolizing the need to eat the Word and drink in the Holy Spirit. Jesus is multifaceted and most often taught in parables. As a result, there are many ways that we can learn of God through the words spoken in the Word. Then in Matthew 4:4, when Satan was trying to tempt Jesus to turn stones to bread, Jesus quotes from Deuteronomy 8:3 that "man shall not live on bread alone, but on every word that comes from the mouth of God!" In Matthew 6:11 in the Lord's/Disciples prayer, it says, "give us today our daily bread."

So, evaluate yourself today as you take the bread and juice of communion. Are you sufficing to eat the flesh and blood randomly, and that is it - because it is not enough? Yes, you have eternal life when you recommit your life, ask forgiveness, and worship Jesus as Lord. But even Jesus said you can not live on that alone, but must have continual communion, hearing the Word of God on a day-by-day, minute-by-minute basis. God knows what you need and will supply it when you stay constantly connected with Him.

As you eat the bread, commit to fellowship continually with Jesus and make the eating of the Word a staple in your daily walk.

Prayer Starter: Lord, forgive me for not recognizing the importance of communion with You, Jesus, and the Holy Spirit. I determine this day to stay in a place of continual communion, reading Your Word daily, taking the time to hear from You as I meditate on Your Word and pray. I realize now that I cannot live by bread alone, but by every Word spoken from Your mouth.

Notes

Day 52
The Cup: Never Thirst Again!
John 4:14, 6, 15:26, 16:7

*J*esus' blood was the D.N.A. (Divine and Natural Authority) we now have because we have given our life to Christ. He shed His Divine and Natural Authority, His D.N.A. here on Earth, taking only the Divine so He could return to the Father in Heaven. When we accept Jesus, we are transfused with His D.N.A. and the Holy Spirit, who God sent once Jesus returned to Heaven (John 15:26; 16:7). As we read in John 6, we are to drink the blood of Jesus. What happens when we drink something? It is filtered throughout our body, permeating every cell. When we drink in the Holy Spirit, a river of the direct connecting/flowing from the throne of God, we will never thirst again (John 4:14).

As you drink from this cup, ask the Holy Spirit to fill you with His life-sustaining, life-giving, refreshing, and quenching presence, power, and life that flows in and through you and connects you to your Heavenly Father and Jesus. Drink all three in!

Prayer Starter: Thank you, Jesus, that You took on the natural body so that by Your death, I would be transfused with Your "D"ivine authority in my natural body. Thank you, God, for sending the Holy Spirit to live in me so that Jesus' "D"ivine nature can flow through me.

Notes

Day 53
The Bread: Full Meal Deal
Deuteronomy 8:3; Matthew 4:4; 1 Corinthians 3:2 (KJV); John 6:47–58

When we sit down to eat, most individuals want a good meat and potato meal, some veggies, some bread, and of course a dessert. We would be happy and healthy and feel loved. What if for a week, maybe a month, or God forbid a year, all we got for every meal was bread? Think about that. Yet this is what Jesus meant when He quoted Deuteronomy 8:3 in Matthew 4:4, "Man shall not live on bread alone, but on every word that comes from the mouth of God." We must be mature and get away from the milk, and on to the meat of the Word, as 1 Corinthians 3:2 (KJV) tells us. We must dig deep into the Word of God to get the potatoes that lie deep in the Word; daily, we must chew on the results (veggies) of the seeds sown and harvested, all of this with Jesus, the Bread of Life (John 6:47–58). As well, drinking in the presence, power, and communion with the Holy Spirit! **ALL** of this is topped off with the most incredible dessert—the sweet presence of the Godhead resting in every one of our senses—bringing joy, happiness, pleasure, sweetness, satisfaction, and so much more! Jesus never meant to be the only part of our meal, our only sustenance. He is part of the full meal deal God has for us.

Prayer Starter: Lord, I pull up my chair to Your table where You serve the FULL MEAL! Holy Spirit, teach me how to dig for the potatoes, chew on the veggies, savor the juicy meat, enjoy the bread, and drink in Your presence. I want to be full from the meals with You, Lord! I am looking forward to enjoying the sweet dessert!

The Cup: Your Blood Does Not Lie!
Mark 2:17; Exodus 15:26;
Isaiah 53:5; Psalm 103:2–3

*W*e must go for routine blood work. Why? Because our blood tells our physician if anything is wrong with us. If we are deficient or overloaded in our body in any way, whether we are in good health or need further testing. What a miraculous design God created that we now know about. However, how often do we check with the Great Physician regarding the health status of our Spiritual blood — the Divine blood that Jesus shed for us and infused into us at our new birth? Are we spiritually anemic? Have we been eating a well-balanced diet of the Word, prayer, and time with the Holy Spirit, Jesus, and God? What about fellowshipping, ministering, and interceding? Every one of these are what we must do to keep our human spirit blood levels equal to the Divine blood levels of Christ so that our spiritual blood system does not get out of whack and require supernatural intervention.

Today, take time to get a human-natural spirit/Holy Spirit blood check by God—the Great Physician. Then do what God says to make sure you are healthy for the walk set before you. Drink from the cup, committing to do whatever the Great Physician has asked of you to ensure your blood levels are where they need to be.

Prayer Starter: Jesus, You are the Great Physician. You shed Your blood so I can have Divine healing. Forgive me for putting all my trust only in earthly physicians when it was You who gave them their ability to have this knowledge. So, I come to You, Lord, for Your wisdom, for my healing. Help me see what is lacking and what I'm overloading myself on so that the spiritual blood You filled me with will not become anemic. Teach me how to tap into the powerful, balanced blood of Jesus.

Day 54
The Bread: True Love
1 John 4:10, 11, 16, 18, 19;
John 3:14–16, 5:24, 14:6, 15:13

On Valentine's Day, the world celebrates love. Human, earthly, physical love, this holiday started as a pagan celebration of Eros love. Most people celebrate numerous events in a year to signify and celebrate love—weddings, anniversaries, birthdays; firsts of this, that, and the other. But for us who know and love God, we celebrate love daily, if not more. Why? Because, as it says in 1st John 4:19, we love Him (God) because He first loved us! 1st John 4 explains the love relationship God has with us. In verse 10, it illustrates how, because of love, God sent Jesus to pay for our sins (John 15:13: Jesus loved us so much that He laid down His life for us). In verse 16, God is love. In verse 18, we learn that there is no fear where God's love is because God's perfect love casts/drives out fear. In verse 11, we are reminded that God loved us, so we should love others.

So today, take this bread to celebrate, as you do every day, the greatest love act that was done for you—Jesus giving His life so you could have authentic, pure, and holy intimacy with your Lord God. Jesus made it possible to spend eternity with the greatest love of your life! Take this bread in remembrance of real, true love.

Prayer Starter: God, You are the love of my life! You made a way for me to spend eternity with You through Your Son, Jesus; I have full access to You. Help me remember that nothing here on Earth compares with Your love. I do not have to wait to have true intimacy, pure intimacy, holy intimacy with You, Lord God. Your love casts out/drives out all fear!

The Cup: The Color Red!
Romans 5:5; Ephesians 3:14–19; John 4:23

*O*h, how interesting it is that the greatest act of love—Jesus dying on the cross—required Jesus to empty himself of all His blood, the blood that covers all our sins. Thus, as God sees us, He only sees the purity and holiness of Jesus. The greatest love—the love of Jesus—is eternal, faithful, honest, not self-serving, and comes from genuine purity. It is a love that moves us to worship, adore, and celebrate every moment of every day.

Lord, let me always remember, You are genuinely and wholly true love whenever I see RED, in remembrance of Jesus' love.

So today, take this cup in remembrance of the ultimate gift of love given by Jesus by laying down His life, pouring out all His blood, and purchasing your life for eternity so you will know the true depth, width, height, and length of genuine love.

Prayer Starter: Jesus, thank you for dying on the cross and shedding Your blood as the ultimate act of LOVE! No holiday or event compares to the love You have shown and given me—a pure and unrelenting love like no other. I love You, Jesus, and I thank You for Your unending love for me.

Day 55
The Bread: God's Grace
Titus 2:11–14; Ephesians 2:8; Zechariah 12:10

*W*e most often relate Jesus's death on the cross as God's grace—His way to reconcile us to Him, thus giving us access to His unmerited favor so we would be made the righteousness of God in and through Jesus. And this is true and amazing and worthy to be celebrated and remembered daily.

However, let's look further into this by going back to the Old Testament, where Jesus was weaved throughout the Word. The word for God's grace in the Old Testament was *chesed*. It denotes deliverance from enemies, affliction, or adversity. It also denotes enablement, daily guidance, forgiveness, and preservation.[13] Take a few minutes and think about how Jesus not only fulfills the unmerited favor/provision of salvation (*charis* grace) of the New Testament but also fulfills the *chesed* grace of the Old Testament.

Over the next few days, we will dig deeper into how Jesus fulfills each of the meanings of *chesed*. Take some time to think about each of these and thank God for each area of grace in your life. As you eat the bread, meditate on how Jesus gave of Himself throughout time just for you.

Prayer Starter: Jesus, thank you for not just providing unmerited favor through Your provision of salvation, but for also providing deliverance from my enemies, deliverance from affliction, and deliverance from adversity. And You don't stop there; You also enable me to do all I need daily through Your minute-by-minute guidance. You continually forgive me when I ask, and You are preserving me in every way. Thank you, Jesus! You are more than enough for me!

---

[13] *https://www.allaboutgod.com/definition-of-gods-grace-faq.htm*

The Cup: Mercy
Romans 6:23; Jeremiah 29:13; John 10:27

God's mercy was given to us when Jesus died for us. Jesus poured all His blood over us to cover us and take our deserved wrath of God that would result in death. Jesus paid our price—death and separation from God. God allowed this so that He could patiently wait for us to come to Him. God's mercy calls us to Him—the price was paid in full by Jesus; it is now a free gift, and God is extending His mercy to us freely. We can run away, hide, deny, whatever. Even still, God continually extends His mercy to us without the need for payment. The only sacrifice we must make, which is no sacrifice, is to walk away from this world and into the loving arms of our Heavenly Father.

Prayer Starter: Thank you, Jesus, for paying the price and covering me with Your blood so God's mercy can freely be extended to me continually.

Listen for the still small voice of God calling to you to rest in the ever-open arms of your Heavenly Father. He is there, inside you, desiring to embrace you with His love if you accept it. As you drink from the cup, drink in the love He has for you.

Day 56
The Bread: Deliverance from Enemies!
Revelation 1:18; Ephesians 6:10–18

*W*ho is our biggest enemy? Satan—he has hated God since he was cast away from the presence of God, and WE who are made in the image of God are a constant reminder to Satan of who he will never be and that he will never be in the presence of God again. When Jesus came, He came to do many things; the most important was to save us. However, Jesus also came to teach and show us how to live, to give us a living example here on earth of God, and to once and for all deliver us from the hand of the enemy—Satan! When Jesus took all our deserved punishment on the cross and then died, He did not stop there. He then took the keys to death and the grave from Satan and rose victorious. We do not have to fight a battle with Satan; the struggle is in us knowing Jesus already won the battle. Jesus lives in us, and the enemy must bow to Jesus' name! Oh yes, the enemy will mount unending attacks, hindrances, oppressions, and more as his demons try to barrage us with the hope that they can find a crack in our armor. BUT, Jesus is our deliverer! When we continually keep our focus on Jesus, putting on HIS ARMOR, no cracks will be found, and when in the heat of battle (when our mind tells us we've lost the battle), moment by moment, we can rest in the fact that because of Jesus we are delivered from our enemies.

Take the bread, savor the protection Jesus' sacrifice provides.

Prayer Starter: Lord, help me put my armor on continually so I can rest in Your *chesed* grace that delivers me from my enemies. Because of you, my armor has no cracks; I am safe in You!

The Cup: Justified
Romans 5:9; Hebrews 4:16; 1 Corinthians 8:6

Justified: 1. To be freed from past sin by PARDON (www.johnsondictionaryonline.com). 2. To declare innocent or guiltless, absolve, acquit (www.dictionary.com). Put these two definitions in place of the justified in Romans 5:9. We can see the power that the blood of Jesus has to save us from the wrath we deserve from God while we were unrepentant sinners who had not accepted Jesus, the gift—God's only Son—who God sent to die for us once and for all. And what power that is in the blood that covered us, even when we were still sinners. This gift opened the door for God to continually extend His mercy and call us into righteousness—right standing with Him through the completed work of the cross that Jesus did for us. So, once we accept Jesus, His death, burial, and resurrection, we are pardoned, declared innocent/guiltless, absolved of any wrongdoing/sin, and acquitted. We are welcomed into an eternal relationship with God.

As you drink from the cup, meditate on the FACT that you are pardoned, declared innocent/guiltless, absolved of all wrongdoing/sin, and acquitted. What does that mean to you? Thank Jesus for justifying you.

Prayer Starter: Thank you, God, that because I accepted Your Son, Jesus, I am pardoned, declared innocent/guiltless, absolved of any wrongdoing/sin, and acquitted. I am justified by the blood of Jesus.

Day 57
The Bread: Deliverance from Affliction
Isaiah 53:4–5

$\mathcal{I}$saiah 53 describes all that Jesus took on himself at the cross. The broad issues include all the issues of life that can afflict us emotionally, physically, psychologically, spiritually, relationally and any other way. We must remember that Jesus took it all for us and wiped the slate clean. Each time we take communion, we can remind ourselves it is not our portion to carry the weight of what Jesus has already paid the price for. Our body, mind, and soul must line up to the will of our Heavenly Father through the completed work of the cross by Jesus and by the Holy Spirit living in us, perfecting us day by day. We have been delivered by the Lamb of God—Jesus—who gave His life to destroy the power of the enemy. He then rose again, renewed. Let every day be a day we also arise renewed and ready to try and succeed.

As you eat the bread, focus on how Jesus bore it all and rose victorious so you can make it through anything and rise victorious in Christ!

Prayer Starter: Thank you, Lord, that Jesus delivered me from ALL my afflictions, every emotionally, physically, psychologically, spiritually, relationally, and in all other ways or afflictions that have held me down. I determine that with Your guidance and help, Holy Spirit, I will rise renewed each day and continue to push forward.

The Cup: The Blood
1 Peter 1:18–19

*I*t seems that genuine respect for and honor OF the blood of Jesus is lacking more and more. People say, "Jesus shed His blood for me" as easily as they say cheeseburger or double caramel mocha! The depth of power in the blood has not changed. Do we still have the awe that once amazed us as to how Jesus' blood did so much for us even as we were still sinners? The blood that has the power to transform, heal, and wash us completely clean from our past, present, and future? Take some time now to think about what the blood of Jesus is to you. Is it power or just a passing phrase?

Prayer Starter: Father, forgive me for neglecting the power and authority within You and for minimizing all that the blood of Jesus includes and has dominion over. Remind me that the blood of Jesus runs through me, Your born-again child!

Day 58
The Bread: Deliverance From Adversity
Isaiah 30:18-23; John 16:33

*A*dversity is the continuous, unending STATE of negative situations and circumstances. Adversity often feels like the "1-2 punch over and over" and is tiring, overwhelming, depressing, and seems to push until we are ready to give up. In the Old Testament in Isaiah 30:18-23, it talks about God's grace, compassion, and justice. In verse 20, it says that although the Lord gives us the bread of adversity and the water of oppression, our Teacher will no longer hide Himself. Our eyes will constantly see our teacher. During the time of the Old Testament, they only had symbols of Jesus. But God knew that He was sending Jesus to deliver us from adversity. In John 16:33, Jesus said that in this world, we will have trouble/adversity, but that we are to take heart. Jesus overcame the world! We now have the teacher spoken of in Isaiah 30:20 who we can constantly look to. Whether the adversity comes from the Lord (which it can in the form of loving discipline) or from the enemy (to buffet us), either way, we have Jesus who delivered us at the Cross and God's Holy Spirit who are our eternal teachers. So, choose to look for and find your teachers, Jesus, and God's Holy Spirit, no matter what you are going through.

Just as real as this bread is in your hand, so is the realness of the love, power, and sound mind that Jesus and God's Holy Spirit can, and will, give you as you go through the adversities of life. Take, eat!

Prayer Starter: Jesus, You know how challenging adversity is. You and God's Holy Spirit are the best teachers to help me through every adversity, big or small. I choose to do as You said in John 16:33 and take heart/be brave/take courage because You overcame and so can I!

The Cup: My Blood Does Not Skip Generations!
Psalm 100:5, 119:90–91, 148:6; 1 John 5:7

So, Jesus and the Holy Spirit are God (Me). We are one! However, many people see only Jesus and the Holy Spirit but neglect how I (God) do not and have never skipped a generation. From Adam to us now, I have been in every generation. My Holy Spirit has been active in every generation, guiding and leading the way, most often through a central leader and in each believer. And Jesus is threaded by types and shadows[14] throughout the Old Testament. I had already preplanned—predestined—when Jesus would come to Earth and what He would do to redeem My people. Jesus would be the spotless and holy sacrifice, so My people would have deliverance from the adversity in this world through the blood of the unblemished lamb and His death, burial, and resurrection! Then Jesus rose victorious, and I sent the Holy Spirit to inhabit My people. Jesus demonstrated how to live and function in this world. Upon His return to Me, I sent My Holy Spirit to give you the POWER to do what I called you to do.

As you hold this cup, think about how Jesus was woven, symbolized, and manifested throughout the Old Testament and up until now. As you drink this cup, know that God never skipped a generation, and He won't skip you either. You are as important to Him as all generations past and to come. Drink from the cup, thanking God for His past, present, and future faithfulness.

---

[14] *For more on Types and Shadows of Jesus through the Old Testament, check out* The Miracle of the Scarlet Thread Expanded Edition: Revealing the Power of the Blood of Jesus from Genesis to Revelation *by Dr. Richard Booker.*

Prayer Starter: Thank you, Lord, for giving us Your Word so we can study and see how faithful you have been throughout all the previous generations and Your faithfulness to me through Jesus and the Holy Spirit. You were with them as you are with me, thank you, Lord, for never leaving me nor forsaking me!

AFFIRMATIONS

Holy Spirit, thank You for Your life-sustaining, life-giving, refreshing, and quenching presence, power, and life that flows in and through me, and connects me to God.

Notes

Day 59
The Bread: Enablement!
John 14:12; Romans 8:38-39; Acts 1:8

*E*nablement: the action of giving someone the authority or means to do something; the action of making something possible.[15] God's *chesed* grace of the Old Testament is that even before Jesus had come to Earth, God gave His grace to those who believed His authority and means to do anything. God made it possible! Then God sent Jesus, who lived every day with the power of God in Him. Jesus was God walking among His people again and demonstrating His *chesed* grace from the Old Testament in New Testament times. God has now given us this same ability because of His Holy Spirit in us, so we are to walk in the same power and authority through our connection to God's *chesed* grace! In John 14:12, Jesus tells us we are to do what He did and even more extraordinary things. Jesus sacrificed Himself on the cross so we would never again be separated from God. He paid the price for our redemption, Divine connection, and full access to God's *chesed* grace, mercy, forgiveness, power—all that God is! Through Jesus and the Holy Spirit, God has enabled us to have authority and means to do great and mighty things for God. God has made this possible for us when we avail ourselves to be used for His glory.

As you take the bread, think about what Jesus did throughout his time on Earth; as you eat the bread, realize God expects you to do even greater things than Him (John 14:12).

Prayer Starter: Thank you, God, for your *chesed* grace and for enabling me to complete all You want me to be and do!

---

[15] *www.on-linedictionary.com*

The Cup: Comforter and Guide!
Mark 13; Philippians 1:6; Matthew 10:20; John 14:26-27, 16:13-14

*J*esus covered us with His blood! When Jesus fulfilled His purpose on Earth through the crucifixion, resurrection, and elevation, He took on all our sins and was a lamb offering/blood sacrifice for us so that He could redeem us to the Father. It was not so we could have an easy, carefree life. No, He did this because He knew what was to come, as He explained in Mark 13. Having provided for our redemption, God then sent the Holy Spirit to be our comforter and guide through all that will occur before Jesus returns. We will need the blood of Jesus (His D.N.A. [Divine and Natural Authority]), God's Holy Spirit, and the assurance that since Jesus remained strong and confident in God making it through the worst of the worst, being crucified, then we to can make it through all we will encounter. We must be confident of God's great love for us, and we are to be actively working and watching at the door for the Master's return. God has enabled us to complete our assigned tasks on Earth. He gave us the Holy Spirit to speak through us in every situation as we stand firm and faithful to the resurrection power of Jesus' Name until the end.

Jesus required the assistance of the Holy Spirit to go through all He did while here on Earth. As you drink the cup in remembrance of Jesus' sacrifice at the cross, realize that even Jesus knew you would need the Holy Spirit, so He accended so God could send Him, the same Holy Spirit who lived in and walked and helped Jesus to live in you. Drink from the cup and thank God for the Holy Spirit and your connection with Jesus because of Him.

Prayer Starter: Lord, thank you for Your Holy Spirit, who is my Comforter and Guide as I complete the plans and purposes You have set for me.

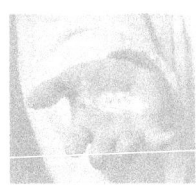

Day 60
The Bread: Daily Guidance
2 Timothy 3:16; John 8:32, 14:26;
1 Corinthians 2:10–11, 3:16; Ephesians 1:17–20

*J*esus provided us with continual guidance in so many ways. He came and dwelled with mankind, lived a holy life, showed us what we are capable of doing in and through God, took and paid the price for our sins, redeeming us when He went to the cross and died for us. Then He resurrected! We now have the Word of God (the Bible) to continually study and get an unending supply of knowledge and guidance. And at His death, the veil was torn, so we have complete access to the Father. Then God made an exchange after Jesus resurrected. Jesus, who was 'God with us,' returned to Heaven, and then God sent His Holy Spirit to be IN us. All this so that we would have an intimate, close relationship with God, through Jesus, and in us by the Holy Spirit, and would have the constant guidance provided by the grace and mercy of a loving Father.

As you look at the bread, think about how you can interact with it (just as Jesus was able to be seen, touched, smelled, etc.). Now you are going to chew it up (just like the destruction of Jesus' body at the crucifixion), you will swallow it (symbolizing Jesus' body going into the grave for three days). Jesus rose (and so do you every time you acknowledge the Holy Spirit in you; you too are revitalized with the authority and power of God Himself!)

Prayer Starter: Thank you, Jesus, for all You did and continue to do, providing me with daily guidance through the Word. Thank you, Holy Spirit, for residing in me and for Your continual guidance within me!

The Cup: Your History
Ephesians 1:5, 13–14, 2:1–13; Galatians 4:4–5; Romans 8:15

It is now known that our blood can give us our history through our DNA. The focus though is on our natural history—where our ancestors came from. However, when we are looking at our supernatural ancestry, the focus changes. Throughout this book, we have been looking at our God-given D.N.A. (Divine and Natural Authority). If the focus were on our "N"atural history, it would be called our NDA, but the D comes first because our focus is on the "D"ivine. This Divine history is most important and is the easiest to research and know because of Jesus. Jesus was conceived in Mary; a human God chose who was obedient, courageous, faithful, and morally pure. The father of Jesus is God, who, through His Holy Spirit, "impregnated" Mary creating Jesus. Being the Son of God, Jesus became the sacrifice, shedding His blood, so that we are adopted into, merged by the blood of Jesus, to be the children of God, rightful heirs with Christ. We can call God our Father! Thus, our Divine history becomes only one generation from God.

As you look at the cup, recognize that you are a direct descendent of God because of what this cup symbolizes—the blood of Jesus. As you take the cup, thank Jesus, and love on God, your Divine Father!

Prayer Starter: Thank you, Jesus, for infusing me with Your D.N.A. so that I am now a direct descendent of the Divine God!

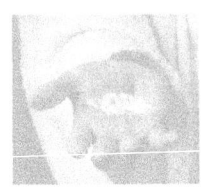

Day 61
The Bread: Forgiveness
Exodus 12:1–20; 1 Peter 1:19; Hebrews 9:14; Galatians 5:13–14

Throughout the Old Testament, God had specific, detailed instructions for the people and priests to complete for His grace to be released. When Jesus went to the cross, having completed all the requirements to be the lamb that was perfect and unblemished, He took on every single sin we would ever commit and paid the price for us so we would be forgiven and covered by the grace of God. Jesus is our forgiveness—His blood covers us and allows God to see perfection when He sees us. When we ask God for forgiveness, God willingly gives it because Jesus already paid the price for it. Our forgiveness was paid for at the cross; we must be willing to come humbly before God and request it in the Name of Jesus. This forgiveness does not give us the liberty to sin. It is way more amazing to ask God's Holy Spirit in us for direction, blessings, intimacy, and connection than having to ask for forgiveness like it was a revolving door. Seek to live in a place of complete forgiveness so you can bask in the presence of God unhindered.

As you bask in the presence of God and feel the Holy Spirit rise within you, recognize this is possible because of all Jesus did. Enjoy the all-encompassing presence. Let this bread represent the sweetness of God's presence because of what Jesus did by giving Himself completely for our redemption.

Prayer Starter: God, I ask in the name of Jesus for Your forgiveness now of anything I have done knowingly or unknowingly that is blocking me from basking in Your presence and growing in my knowledge and understanding of You, Your Kingdom, and Your power in me because of Jesus and through Your Holy Spirit.

The Cup: Transfusion Time!
1 John 3:24; 1 Corinthians 11:27–32; Hebrews 5:11–14

*W*hy are we doing this process of taking communion daily? Because for many, the belief is that "I got born again, Jesus covered all my sins—now I'm good." But the truth is that was just the placement of the needle for the blood transfusion of Jesus' blood—Jesus' D.N.A. (Divine And Natural Authority). We will forever be attached to the IV as the process of transformation takes place. So, each day we get to make sure the needle is still in place, that the Holy Spirit flushes the vein allowing for a faster, more efficient transfusion rate.

If we neglect our need for cleansing by the blood of Jesus, we become spiritually anemic.[16] It shows as spiritual fatigue, a lack of vivid color and clarity in our life both spiritually and naturally, decreased ability to breathe in the breath of God that fills our lungs with air that exhales as His power, we may feel confused or like we are floating on a cloud, and we may have fear and anxiety. How do you avoid this? By, daily, making sure you are continually and adequately being infused with the cleansing blood of Jesus. As you drink from the cup, let it symbolize the beginning of the transfusion taking place in the Spirit right now.

Prayer Starter: Lord, forgive me for neglecting my transfusions or, even worse, for removing the IV that I need to be able to receive Your transfusion. I sit myself down NOW so that I can have my IV checked. I ask that Your Holy Spirit flush the IV, and I STOP, RELAX, and ENJOY the transfusion. I desperately need the D.N.A. (Divine And Natural Authority) that is only found in and through the blood of Jesus!

---

[16] *https://markmayberry.net/wp-content/uploads/bible-study/2007-03-04-pm-MM-SpiritualAnemia.pdf* Spiritual Anemia *by Mark Mayberry 3/4/2007*

Day 62
The Bread: Preservation
Isaiah 53:4-5; Romans 6:11-13; Acts 13:35-37

*W*ebster's dictionary defines preservation[17] as the activity or process of keeping something valued alive, intact, or free from damage or decay. Jesus paid for our preservation! He, out of an undefinable amount of love for us, gave Himself, took on all the pain, agony, and death so that in that, and then in rising from the dead, we would be covered by His blood. God's grace would be extended to us, and we God's children would be preserved. God wanted us whom He loves and values more than we could ever comprehend alive; not dead IN sin but dead TO sin and alive to God in Christ. Even though it may look like life has beat us while we were down, God's Holy Spirit is fully intact within us and has the power and ability to transform the situation. The broken skin that poured out Jesus' blood took the damage we deserved. And just as Jesus did not decay in the grave, Jesus dying, not decaying, and rising gave us access to eternal life where we will never decay. This inability to decay counts for our salvation, our ministry, our life, every area. Taking this time of communion daily is one of the many ways of helping us to remember all Jesus did and continues to do for us.

Take a few moments to think back to all the times when you were preserved from what could or should have happened. Ask the Holy Spirit to bring to remembrance those times that you may not have realized or acknowledged how you were kept alive, intact, and free from damage. As you take the bread, thank Jesus for making it possible for you to be preserved.

---

[17] *https://www.merriam-webster.com/dictionary/preservation*

Prayer Starter: Jesus, thank you for all You did to preserve me in every area of my life!

Journaling

List times when you knew, or are now realizing that God preserved you.

_____

_____

_____

_____

_____

_____

_____

_____

_____

_____

_____

THE D.N.A. OF COMMUNION

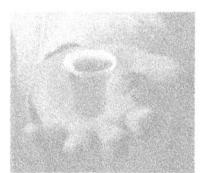

Day 62
The Cup: Cover You With My Blood!
2 Corinthians 5:21; Colossians 1:20

𝑀erriam-Webster defines **cover**[18] numerous ways. Today we will look at one way: to guard from attack, protect/secure, to guard against an opponent's play, to be in a position to receive, to make provision for a demand or charge, to maintain a check/watching over.

The blood of Jesus covers us. Jesus' blood guards us from attack; it protects us, secures us in Him, guards us against Satan's schemes and plans, and allows us to be able to receive from God. Jesus' blood makes provision for every demand on us, for every charge against us. The blood of Jesus keeps us in the ever-watching view of God, and it marks us as with a spotlight as one whom God maintains a constant check and watch.

Take some time to meditate on each of these ways that the blood of Jesus protects you. Drink from the cup in remembrance of this and with gratitude and thankfulness for Jesus and the blood He willingly shed for your redemption.

Prayer Starter: WOW, Jesus!!! I honestly never realized how much Your blood covering me does! Forgive me for relegating it to just redeeming me! Lord, open the eyes of my understanding to comprehend all the blood of Jesus does for me!

---

[18] *https://www.merriam-webster.com/dictionary/cover*

Day 63
The Bread: Barabbas
Romans 5:6–11; Deuteronomy 32:36;
Hebrews 9:22; 1 Thessalonians 1:10

*W*e cannot look at Jesus's crucifixion without looking at the process it took to get there. Many skim over Barabbas being released so Jesus could be crucified, and yet everything happened for a reason. Have we ever truly realized Barabbas <u>was found guilty</u> for what Jesus was falsely being accused of—insurrection of the people? So, Jesus took on Barabbas' charges, thereby pardoning Him; and Jesus did this because He knew it was part of God's plan. Barabbas did not say "thank you," did not turn and become a disciple; he was pardoned and went on with his life. In Romans 5:8, God demonstrated His love for us in this: while we were still sinners, Christ died for us. How many of us take for granted that Jesus died for us even before we gave our lives to Him? No matter what we had done previously, Jesus took the charges and wiped the slate clean. When we accept Jesus as our Lord and Savior, He pays all our debts to the Highest Judge, ALMIGHTY GOD! We get to walk in complete freedom of <u>ALL the charges against us!</u> We get an "adjudication withheld." We were guilty as charged, but the judge does not convict us of our charge for the crimes (sins) committed. Completion of our probationary requirement (repenting) will allow the crimes (sins) to be covered (by the blood of Jesus), resulting in a dismissal of the conviction. Eat the Bread of Expungement of all your wrongs that Jesus provided you when He died and rose for you.

Prayer Starter: Jesus, thank you for being my Savior, Redeemer, and Lawyer. For expunging my habitual record of wrongs. Help me, Holy Spirit, to never forget or take for granted, as Barabbas did, what Jesus did for me. Thank you, Judge Almighty God, for choosing not to remember my wrongs that are covered by the blood of Jesus!

The Cup: Cover me!
Psalm 32:1; 85:2; 1 Peter 4:1-11; Philippians 3:13; Romans 8:1; Hebrews 8:12

Today, let's look at another meaning of **cover** to discover what the blood of Jesus does for us.

Cover: to hide from sight or knowledge (conceal), to lie over (envelop), to lay or spread something over (overlay), to spread over, to appear here and there on the surface of, to place or set a cover or covering over.

The blood of Jesus covers our sins (past-present-future), hiding them from sight or knowledge. We are concealed in the blood — when God looks at us, He sees the blood of Jesus, not our sin. We must take our sin to God, repent in the Name of Jesus, and then we are forgiven. Picture in your mind a large blanket laid over you as you stand there (representing the blood of Jesus); you are completely covered (from the top of your head to the soles of your feet). When you look in any direction, all you see is the blanket (blood). What is behind you, next to you, and in front of you is unseen because of the blanket (the blood of Jesus). When we focus on what is outside of that covering and judge ourselves on those things, we must remove the cover to do this. Do not be fooled into removing your cover of protection by focusing on or looking at what is outside of the blood covering you that you are under.

What have you removed your covering to re-look at or to re-visit? What have you received forgiveness for that you keep trying to pull back inside your blanket of forgiveness to convince God, yourself, or others of your unworthiness? Now, take a moment to ask Jesus to show you, help you let it go, and then help you put it in its rightful place. Ask the Holy Spirit to help you leave it there, and now take the cup to symbolize this.

Prayer Starter: Jesus, thank you for covering me. Forgive me for removing Your covering to look at, re-visit, re-live, return to, or dwell on those things You have covered me from. Help me to choose to forget those things, just as God has chosen to forget them.

Journaling

Make a list of what you have repented for that now is covered under the blood, but you keep trying to remove the covering. Ask God to guide you through the process of forgiving yourself so that you stop focusing on those issues.

_____

_____

_____

_____

_____

_____

YOUR GOD-GIVEN DIVINE & NATURAL AUTHORITY

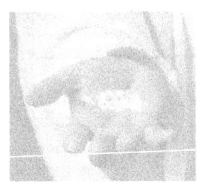

Day 64
The Bread: Mental Anguish
Matthew 27:27–31/Mark 15:16–20;
Ephesians 6:17; Philippians 4:7; Isaiah 26:3

In Matthew 27:27–31/Mark 15:16–20, one of the first ways Jesus was attacked was in/on His head. The soldiers stripped Jesus, put a robe on Him, then put a crown of thorns on His head. After mocking Jesus and spitting on Him, they struck Jesus on the head with the staff again and again while the crown of thorns dug into His scalp and the blood poured from His head. Interestingly, when putting on the Armor of God, we are told to put on the helmet of salvation, which is what Jesus did for us. It was the first thing that Jesus had done to Him, just as it is the first step in our walk with God. Think about that! So the process of Jesus shedding His blood and giving His body as the final sacrifice on the cross started with an attack on His head/mind. This attack against our minds is symbolic because our minds are the battlefield that constantly needs renewing even now. We must reject the enemy's lies attacking us with doubts, unbelief, and conscious and unconscious thoughts. Jesus went through this portion of the anguish to show us/symbolize that He took on all the mental anguish we will have so He can cover it with the blood that poured from his head. Jesus paid the price. So give your mind, your thoughts, and your mental anguish and pain to Jesus today.

Jesus knows and thoroughly understands how the mind can be attacked. As you take the bread, recognize that He did not leave what you are going through unaddressed.

Prayer Starter: Jesus, I plead the blood You shed from Your brow as the crown of thorns dug into you over my mind. The chaos and anguish that has kept me broken and confused, I give it all to You now! In Jesus name!

The Cup: Incubated!
Luke 1:35; 2 Timothy 1:14; Jeremiah 29:11

*a*nother definition of **COVER** is related to birthing our God-designed purpose and destiny. Webster's dictionary defines *cover*[19] as to copulate with (a female) and sitting on and incubating (such as eggs).

God's Holy Spirit covered Mary "copulating with a female" to create Jesus, who Mary incubated in her womb while remaining a virgin—pure! Jesus had to shed His blood to cover us; He resurrected with a renewed eternal body—returned to Heaven, and the Holy Spirit was sent to live within us. The blood of Jesus covers us; the Holy Spirit is in us, and out from that is birthed the power to fulfill the purpose and destiny God put in us. We speak of being pregnant with purpose and destiny and giving birth to it. Our destiny is not possible without the impregnating of purpose, plans, visions, and dreams by God and through the covering and incubation process that the blood of Jesus provides.

As you take the cup today, meditate on the blood of Jesus covering you to incubate that which God impregnated you with. It is impossible to fulfill your purpose and destiny without the blood of Jesus covering you.

Prayer Starter: Jesus, thank you that Your blood covers me, and the Holy Spirit sits within me, and both are needed to incubate what God filled me with so that I can birth His purpose, plan, and destiny.

---

[19] *https://www.merriam-webster.com/dictionary/cover*

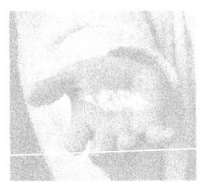

Day 65
The Bread: Let Jesus Be Your Simon!
Matthew 27:26, 16:24-26; Mark 15:15, 21; Genesis 22:6

*J*esus gave us His all! He took all our sin on Himself! He was torn to shreds, taking on what we deserved! Then He carried the cross with His gouged, raw, and bleeding open flesh! He bore the weight of our sins and carried our burdens as He carried the cross. When the centurions believed Jesus had reached the point of exhaustion, the centurions called for Simon of Cyrene to take the cross and carry it the rest of the way to Golgotha. Jesus had to willingly accept Simon's help because Jesus would have pressed on to the mark of His higher calling. Simon's role will be expounded on over the next few days, but for today, Jesus wants us to know He willingly carried the burden of the cross on the wounds of our brokenness, sins, and hurt/pain so that we would not have to. Yes, we are to be like Christ, but even Christ had to allow Simon to take the cross and carry the burden for Him. In being Christlike, do not believe the lie that we alone must carry the cross (yes, Jesus says for us to take up our cross daily and follow Him [Matthew 16:24–26]), but when the burden is too much, and we can't bear it, Jesus is more than willing to carry the cross for us. Allow Jesus to be your Simon.

As you take the bread, think about the shape Jesus' body was in when He had to carry the cross that He would die on. He understands far more than you can comprehend how difficult it is to carry your cross, so yield to Him NOW as you take the bread!

Prayer Starter: Jesus, I know that in Matthew 16:24–26 You said if I want to follow You, I must deny myself, take up my cross and follow You; but sometimes I don't know how to carry the burdens of my cross, and I want to give up. Right now, I ask You to help me as I let You be my Simon.

The Cup: Simon Was The Last And The First!
Mark 15:21; Psalm 38:4, 68:19; Galatians 6:2

*W*hen Simon took the cross, there is no doubt that the blood of Jesus was all over the cross. Simon was the last to help our Lord Jesus, and he was the first to be covered by the blood of Jesus! Jesus demonstrated unrelenting, enduring, and compassionate love through this process, the love ONLY God has the capacity to give. Jesus desires to take our burdens. He knows what comes with it! Our crosses/burdens are covered in all our stress, anxiety, fear, doubt, unbelief, hate, anger, rebellion, and all the negatives, but Jesus understands, and still, He takes it willingly. Simon played an important part in Jesus completing His purpose, and Jesus wants to do for us what Simon did for Him. He carried the burden (regardless of the "mess") and made it possible for Jesus to do it for us as well. With all its "mess," what burden do you need to give to Jesus for Him to carry so you too can fulfill your purpose.

As you hold this cup in your hand, know that Jesus is willing to carry your burdens, your crosses, and He will cover them with His blood.

Prayer Starter: Oh Jesus, I relinquish to You my crosses/burdens that are weighing me down, exhausting me, and are covered in my mess. Even You needed Simon to carry Your cross for some of the distance to fulfill Your purpose. Thank you, Jesus, for carrying mine!

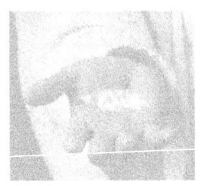

Day 66
The Bread: Cross To Bear!
Matthew 16:24-26, 35-44; Mark 15:29-32; Luke 23:34-43; John 19:23-27

*W*hen Jesus was crucified, nailed to the cross, there was no way for Him to physically fight the vulnerability, humiliation, neglect, abandonment, violation, exposure, judgment, ridicule, and jeering. He could only look out and see the anger, evil, and rejection of those against Him and the sadness, broken hearts, disappointment, and fear of those who loved Him. The list of emotions, thoughts, feelings, etc., is endless. All He could do was cry out in prayer to God. He did not act out in anger; on the contrary, He prayed for all of them. He asked God to 'forgive them, for they knew not what they were doing.' He made sure His mother was taken care of. He exuded love amidst the most horrendous experience ever known.

He did it for us! He took on the worst of the worst! However, in Matthew 16:24-26, Jesus exhorted His followers to take up their cross daily to be His disciples. What burdens are you carrying? What cross do you feel you cannot escape from that makes you experience any of the above emotions? Go to God in prayer—Jesus, your advocate, is there to walk you through to victory. He went through all of that to show us that He CAN CARRY THE HEAVY LOAD! That He took it all on Himself for us. He took on the unbearable, what we think will kill us, and rose again to show us we will make it through.

As you prepare to take the bread, ask Jesus to show you what you must forgive, what you need to give to Him, and how to die to self so that you too can rise victorious as Jesus did.

Prayer Starter: Jesus, You know what it is like to experience all the emotions you dealt with while on the cross. Help me, Jesus, to walk through this, die to self, and rise victorious as You did.

Journaling

What is Jesus showing you that you must forgive, what you need to give to Him, and how to die to self so that you too can rise victorious as He did?

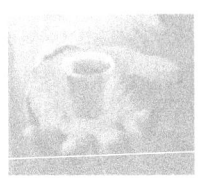

Day 66
The Cup: Legacy-Making!
Mark 15:21; Romans 16:13

Think about Simon—he carried the cross of Jesus, with Jesus' blood covering Him, for an innocent man who would be nailed to it. God planned for Simon to be right there so the Centurions would force him to carry the cross. Simon played a crucial role in God's plan and purpose. Like Simon, we may not always understand how what we are made to, are asked to, or "happen" to be chosen to do will matter. It may seem like a need that is not positive or glamorous. However, in the process, we find that we will be covered in the anointing, blessing, and power of the blood of Jesus just as Simon was. Imagine the effect it had on Simon and on his sons[20] who were with him, and the impact throughout future generations because Simon was the one who carried the cross. The legacy created at that moment became the demonstration/description of the impact of taking up our cross daily and how God will bless us with the anointing and power given to us through the blood of Jesus and God's Holy Spirit.

Recognize as you hold this cup that represents Jesus' legacy of unconditional LOVE and Redemption that you too are part of God's plan, Jesus' legacy, and that as you commit and obey God, you too will leave a legacy. Drink from the cup as a commitment to do whatever God asks you to do.

---

[20] *In Mark 15:21, Alexander and Rufus are named. They are the children of Simon who had to watch their father carry Jesus' cross. Alexander is not spoken of again in the Bible. However, in Romans 16:13, Paul calls Rufus an outstanding Christian, a chosen one of God, selected by God, the elect of God. The effect of watching this scenario occur affected him and demonstrated the legacy left by Simon.*

Prayer Starter: Jesus, sometimes I do not understand why I have to do things, why I am the one chosen, and may even be frustrated that what I have been asked to do is not "positive," "fun," or if it will even matter. I may not realize my role in Your Plan, Lord, but in my obedience, I ask You to use me to leave a legacy.

Notes

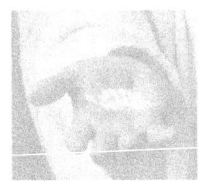

Day 67
The Bread: Always Ready!
Luke 23:40–43; 2 Timothy 4:2; John 14:12–14

While Jesus was hanging on the cross, near-death, He experienced the pain, the anguish, truly incomprehensible agony that of which we have never had to experience and hopefully never will. And even at that moment, Jesus was still ministering when one of the criminals asked Jesus, after defending Jesus when the other criminal hurled insults, to remember Him when Jesus came into His Kingdom! Jesus answered Him, "Truly, I tell you, today you will be with Me in paradise." No matter what Jesus went through, He was always ready and willing to minister. Jesus demonstrated what He wants from us, to be ready to preach/teach the message of Jesus at any time (2 Timothy 4:2). We are to do what Jesus did and even greater things (John 14: 12–14). What stops you from being ready? Ask Jesus how to be bold, focused, ready, and able to minister no matter what situation you are in.

If you are truly ready to be used by Jesus, the one symbolized by this bread in your hand, then commit to open yourself (as you open your mouth) for Jesus to work in and through you (take and eat the bread) now.

Prayer Starter: Lord, help me be ready in season and out of season to speak what You want to be said. Lord, like Jesus, give me the strength to put myself to the side regardless of what is happening to be used by You to meet the needs of the one you have brought before me. I cannot do it without You, without Your Holy Spirit, and without the power and anointing from Jesus.

The Cup: Blood & Water = Holy Spirit
1 John 5:6–12 (Living Bible); John 19:34, 7:37–39

In 1 John 5:8, three witnesses on earth declare that *Jesus Christ is the Son of God*. The first is the voice of the Holy Spirit in our hearts. Second is the voice from Heaven (God) who said so when John had baptized Christ. And lastly, the voice of the blood of Jesus before He died. (The Living Bible)

John 19:34 talks about the soldier piercing Jesus' side with a spear, thereby bringing a sudden flow of blood and water, causing, physically, the complete demonstration of Jesus being emptied of His blood/D.N.A. (Divine and Natural Authority) and His water, as John 7:37–39 states that the water was the Holy Spirit leaving Jesus. Why? Because soon the Holy Spirit would be released on the earth in full measure and into everyone who believes in Jesus, the Holy Spirit would be empowered and fully activated.

Jesus gave Himself so that you would be able to be adopted into God's family. You were born with the Holy Spirit in you, but when you accepted Jesus, the Holy Spirit was activated, becoming more active in your life.

Prayer Starter: Lord, thank you for sending Jesus to pay the sacrifice so that the Holy Spirit would reside with me and that when I accept Your Son, the Holy Spirit within me is activated and emboldened and able to function at the full measure He always was but was restrained from demonstrating.

Day 68
The Bread: Car Care
1 Corinthians 6:12–20

When we have a car, we treat it better and take better care of it than we do the vehicle the Holy Spirit uses. Our cars transport us, so we don't have to walk, carry our burdens and us/and our family, take us places, and cover us. They require gas and/or electricity, regular maintenance to function properly, and we will wash the outside and clean the inside. Our cars get dinged, dented, and can save or even kill us in a crash. We get in and use it over and over every day. For some, it is a status symbol, and everyone has their preferences based on their needs and wants. We take great care of our car because we cannot imagine life without it, and it is devastating and practically stops our life from functioning if we do not have a car. Our kids beg us for one, and we get them one.

So, why do we neglect the only vehicle God, our creator and giver of life, has to function in this world? Think about what we do for our car—do we do even half as much for God's vehicle—US?!

God's vehicle will be the focus for the next few days.

Prayer Starter: Father, forgive me for not caring for the only physical vehicle You have to do Your work here on Earth. Lord, help me see what I need to do to ensure that Your vehicle is properly cared for.

The Cup: Let This Cup Pass!
Matthew 26:39, 42, 44

When Jesus prayed in the garden of Gethsemane, He went because He knew He needed His father. He was overwhelmed with sorrow to the point of death. During the first prayer, He asked God, "If it is possible, may this cup be taken from me. Yet, not as I will, but as You will!" What does a cup do? It holds something. Our body is a cup that holds the D.N.A. (Divine and Natural Authority) of God, God's Holy Spirit, and can hold any liquid or solid to measure, store, consume, or share. So, in this first prayer, Jesus asked God if it was possible that His cup/body could be taken from Him. It is unknown if God answered Jesus in silence, a knowing, or in an audible voice. But we know what Jesus says, "Yet not as I will (to not go through the process of crucifixion) but as You (Lord, Father, God) will. Jesus, like us, needed to ask God, "Are you sure?" Even though He knew the answer.

Tomorrow we will look at the second prayer.

Prayer starter: Lord, I know I ask many times, "Why Lord?" "Do I really have to go through this?" "Isn't there some other way?" Help me hear Your heart even if it is in the silence, through Your Holy Spirit the still and quiet voice in me, or audibly through others speaking Your words. Help me, Lord, to get to the place of "not my will, but Yours."

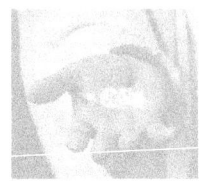

Day 69
The Bread: Transports
Romans 8:2, 9, 11, 23; John 14:17

𝒲e are the transport body for God's Holy Spirit to move, act, and do His will in this world. When we transition to realizing our life is not our own, the cares of this world have less pull on us. God provided us a body to do His will while living and maneuvering in this world.

When we have a car—a vehicle—it transports/carries us where we need and want to go. With that vehicle, we can carry burdens—heavy to light and our families, friends, pets, etc. It keeps us safe from the elements and allows us to continue moving forward in our mission and purpose. Think about this: we are the vehicle God uses to carry Him/His Holy Spirit wherever He wants and needs to go. We can carry His burdens and blessings. We are responsible for taking care of our bodies so we can keep the Holy Spirit safely protected and continue moving forward in God's mission and purpose. Jesus demonstrated this to us by coming and walking among us to fulfill God's purpose.

What an honor it is to know you carry the Lord's burdens and the Lord's answers through His Holy Spirit. It is not about you, how good you can or do look; it is about being all you can be so that God will be able to work in and through you to do His will in this Earth and with everyone He puts in your path.

Prayer Starter: Lord, You provided me with this body to be a transport of all You are while I am here on Earth. Help me see what I need to do to maintain it to do what You need me to do.

The Cup: Drink It!
Matthew 26:42; Luke 22:39–46

𝒯he second prayer Jesus prayed demonstrates the progress of conversation with God and acceptance by Jesus. In Matthew 26:42, Jesus prayed, "My Father, if it is NOT possible for this cup (body) to be taken away unless I drink it (suffering/crucifixion), may Your will be done!" Luke 22:39–46 says God sent an angel from Heaven to Jesus to strengthen Him. Jesus then prayed more earnestly to the point that His sweat was drops of blood falling to the ground. Jesus was interceding for Himself and pressing into the will of God. The dripping blood symbolized the intensity of Jesus' intercession and foretold of the bloodshed from His head for our salvation. This second prayer was the acceptance of what must be done. The angel Luke spoke of who God sent strengthened not only Jesus' body but also His human spirit, resolve, determination, and purpose to do the will of His Father. The first prayer was to line up His body to God's plan; the second one was to line up His human will to God's will so that God's purpose on Earth could be done.

Jesus knew that God's will was for Him to die on the cross so that all would have redemption unto God. However, the human side of Jesus had to be prepared for what this would require. Often, when you want to give up, it is imperative to go to God so that He can minister to you and give you the strength to push on and through what is to come. Then together, you and God can celebrate what He brought you through. He will always turn everything for good, even if it feels miserable while going through it.

Prayer starter: God, where in my life do I need to line up to You in my body and my will so that I can fulfill what You need me to do?

Day 70
The Bread: What is Significant!
John 10:10, Romans 8:29

*W*hen we think about a car, it is not the car that is significant. Just look at all the car lots worldwide and even the junkyards—millions and millions of unused vehicles. The cars are only significant if they are filled with precious cargo; thus, the vehicle becomes valued because of what is inside and the purpose held in it. So too with us! Our body, the vehicle chosen by God to live in, holds the precious cargo of the Holy Spirit, purpose, plans, etc., within it. The world focuses on the vehicle—what it looks like externally. Unfortunately, this is often at the expense of the cargo inside. For many, their focus is on whether they are driving a Ferrari or an old beat-up clunker. However, there is one HUGE difference between us and a car: we only get one body—we cannot purchase an upgrade as we can for a car. Thus the Lord wants us to do the maintenance both physically and internally to have this vehicle for the predestined amount of time and not be taken out by the devil's desire and plan to kill, steal, and destroy us.

What your vehicle "looks like" is less important than being primed and ready for full action, participation, and to be used by God.

Prayer Starter: Lord, thank you for the body You gave me! Forgive me for where I have neglected to care properly for Your vehicle and have disregarded the precious cargo You placed within me. Help me, Lord, to focus not on the look of the vehicle but on the function of the vehicle so that I can fulfill Your purpose and plan for my life.

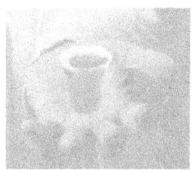

The Cup: Being Resolved!
Matthew 26:35, 41, 43-44

Jesus knew the weakness of mankind. Just as He said to Peter, "pray that you will not be tempted." Tempted by what? To do his own will and not God's will, Jesus knew Peter wanted to do what was right. Still, Peter was weak and often fell into his own will, as demonstrated by not even being able to stay awake for one hour to be on the watch for Jesus, even though in verse 35 Peter said, "I will die with you!"

Then Jesus went the second time to pray and submitted His human will to God's will. When He came back, and all three were again asleep, Jesus did not even wake them. He just left them to go back and pray a third time. Verse 43-44.

He went the third time to align with the will of His Father, being 100% in agreement that He had to drink the cup of suffering for the sake of humans. He knew they wanted to do the right thing but were too weak to do it without Him bearing the brunt of the full measure of their weakness. The resolve Jesus returned with after the third prayer gave Jesus the motivation, strength, and courage to bear the weight of suffering required to redeem all people to God.

What also do you need to go to God about so that you can get into agreement 100% and be filled with the same type of motivation, strength, and courage to bear the weight of what God has for you, just as He did for Jesus?

Prayer Starter: Jesus, thank you for taking on the full measure of my human weakness. I often desire to do what You ask of me, but I cannot do it in my weakness. I am so grateful, Jesus, that You paid the price for me to have Your strength, motivation, and courage to do what is asked of me. I am not alone!

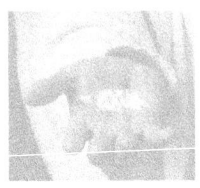

Day 71
The Bread: Maintenance
1 Corinthians 2:10, 3:16, 6:19–20; Titus 3:5; Acts 1:8; Galatians 5:22–23

*W*ith our cars, we must get maintenance done to ensure that they run well to get as many years as possible out of them. We do not want to break down anywhere because we have neglected to care for our car. Nor do we desire to put our precious cargo at any risk. Yet, how often do we make sure to get God's vehicle's maintenance done?

We have been provided through the knowledge God provides in his Word and through medical professionals to maintain a healthy physical body. To keep the maintenance up in our physical/spiritual body, we need water/the Holy Spirit, oil/the anointing, gas or electric/the Word, engine maintenance/power, tire checks/prayer, an electrical system/communication with/between the Lord/Jesus/Holy Spirit and all systems. And for us to have a clear and safe drive, we must regularly replace the washer fluid and windshield wipers/renew the mind to be able to see clearly, differently, and better.

Now, to maintain a healthy spiritual vehicle (which holds the precious cargo, the Holy Spirit, and our destiny and purpose), to do the will of the Father in this world, we must daily do these relational maintenance responsibilities. When we let one area go, it will influence the whole vehicle's ability to do what it is designed to do.

Prayer starter: Lord, I will stop at the Holy Spirit maintenance shop every day for a tune-up so that I will be a well-maintained vehicle for You. I am so glad Your Holy Spirit is thorough and that Jesus has already paid the bill!

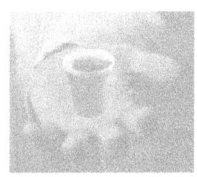

The Cup: All Must Drink
Matthew 26:27, 39, 42, 44

𝒥n Matthew 26:27, Jesus tells the disciples, "All of you drink from the cup." In verses 39, 42, and 44, Jesus prayed to His Father not to drink the cup. Then for the second and third prayers, He prayed for God's will to be done since He knew the cup could not be taken away. Jesus chose to drink the cup and shed His blood so that we would not have to. He chose to take on the suffering, shed every ounce of His blood so that when we drink from the cup, we remember that we have a new promise because of Jesus' sacrifice. We can freely drink, and our sins are forgiven. We can boldly go to the throne of God, approaching God as a pure, white-as-snow child of God who has been covered by the blood of the lamb, Jesus.

Think about it, Jesus CHOSE to take on the suffering for you. So, you can have all—not just some of the blessings of God, but all of them.

Prayer Starter: Thank you, Jesus, that as I take this cup, I am doing it in remembrance of what You did so that I am forgiven of my sins, have open access to God, and am pure and holy in God's sight because of the blood You shed. Thank you for the MOST IMPORTANT GIFT ever given to me!

Day 72
The Bread: Keeping Healthy!
James 1:8; Matthew 6:33; Proverbs 3:5–6

𝒟o we do what we need to keep our physical body healthy and functioning as well as possible? Do we go to the Great Physician (God), to His medical servants (medical professionals), and do we eat right, exercise, take vitamins, and medications as we are told to? Yet, this physical/"N"atural is only one part of the D.N.A. (Divine and Natural Authority) that we were given in Christ. The "N" (Natural) is in second place. The "D" comes first and must be healthy for the "N" (Natural) and the "A" (Authority) to be able to function at full capacity.

To review our D.N.A. (Divine and Natural Authority) is the Divine and natural authority/anointing. When we take care of ourselves physically/naturally before we take care to connect with the "D"ivine God, we set ourselves up for an unhealthy "N"atural and thus a weakened level of "A"uthority and "A"nointing. Our DNA must be in proper alignment to function as God desires every moment of our lives.

When we reverse this, we are left with "AND"—a life with no demonstration of God because we sought "A"nointing and "A"uthority in the flesh/"N"atural, leaving no room for the "D"ivine! Thus, we are "AN" unhealthy individual who is unstable in all their ways! James 1:8

Prayer Starter: Lord, help me to focus on the "D"ivine first! I want Your D.N.A., not my AND! Show me, Lord, where I have misdirected what You have given me and put me back on the path that You designed for me.

The Cup: (D)ivine Health is our Standard
1 Corinthians 11:24-30; 2 Timothy 2:15; John 15:7-11

𝒥n the science/medical world, our DNA is evaluated as the cause of illnesses, our traits, and what determines who we are. There are tests that can be run to determine our risk for issues based on our genes. Unfortunately, this only looks at the (N)atural part of the DNA. However, when we accept Jesus as Lord of our lives, the (D)ivine part of our D.N.A. is activated, and it has higher (A)uthority than the (N)atural.

When we access the power and authority of the blood of Jesus by abiding in His Spirit (drinking from the cup that symbolizes His blood) and assimilating His Word (symbolized by eating the bread/His flesh) through communion, we can walk in the health that God has granted us through the completed work of Jesus. Through Jesus' blood, we can walk in Divine health.

Science has yet to discover all that is in the genes and chromosomes that make up our traits. They know only one part because science only can explain the (N)atural portion. The (D)ivine portion is controlled by God and is only changed and understood through the Holy Spirit, Jesus, and the supernatural (A)uthority given to us through our (D)ivine Father God.

You see, for those who have not accepted Jesus as their Lord and Savior, they are bound by the norms of this world, but as a child of God, we are bound by the norms of God's Kingdom. However, this requires us to study to show ourselves approved by looking to God's Word for what is "normal" in His Kingdom. It is abnormal for believers to be weak, fearful, depressed, grieved, or sick. However, due to a lack of knowledge, many of

God's people have accepted the world's standards/norms; thus, they are walking far below their Kingdom privileges.

So, as you take the cup, ask God to illuminate through His Holy Spirit and His Word those things that are only (D)ivinely understood. That as you abide/remain in Him and His Word abides/remains in you, ask whatever you will, and it shall be done for you, including healing from anything the (N)atural part of your DNA tries to put on you.

Prayer Starter: Lord, forgive me for accepting the world's standards and norms regarding my health. Help me understand through Your Holy Spirit and assimilate and take in Your Word so that I can walk in Divine health. Show me through Your Word what privileges I have as a child of the living God. Help me understand how to live by Kingdom standards, not earthly standards, in Jesus' name.

Notes

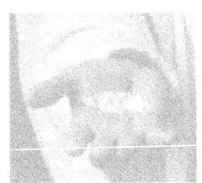

Day 73
The Bread: Washed and Cleaned!
Hebrews 10:22; Matthew 23:25-28[21]

*W*hen we clean our automobiles, we wash the outside and clean the inside. Wash denotes the use of water and soap, so to clean/scrub/rinse/dry is not something we would do inside the car. Inside, we clean, meaning vacuum, dust, throw away the trash and organize. Once those two tasks, both inside and outside, are done, we call our car clean.

One can wash the outside, and yet it is dirty inside; although this observation is not as easily recognized unless one sees or gets inside, the assumption is made that if the outside is clean, the inside must be clean as well. Or one can spotlessly clean the inside, and outside it is dirty; and with an assumption of disgust, it is assumed that the inside is probably just as dirty. Neither of these "assumptions" are accurate. Once cleaned inside and out, it does not remain permanently clean—with use, it gets dirty again and again, requiring cleaning internally and externally repeatedly. The more use, the more attention to keeping it clean is required. How do we do this spiritually? In Hebrews 10:22, it states that the blood of Jesus washes us, we have been washed by salvation; and when we get dirty, as we will, we have a car wash called repentance that we can go to anytime we need.

Prayer Starter: Lord, thank you. When the outside of me gets dirty or the inside of me needs cleaning, I can come to You, repentant, and know that the blood of Jesus washes me clean.

---

[21] *Additional scriptures about being clean and washed:* **CLEAN** – *Matthew 23:26; Acts 10:15, 11:9; 2 Timothy 2:21; Hebrews 9:14, 22; 2 Peter 1:9;* **WASHED** *– 1 Corinthians 6:11; Revelation 7:14; Psalm 73:13*

The Cup: Purity
Romans 5:9; Isaiah 1:18; 1 Corinthians 1:30, 4:3–4

*J*esus' blood represents the purity we have when we come before the Lord. Jesus shed His blood so that we would be pure—white as snow when we stand before God. When God looks at us, He sees the blood of Jesus, which purifies us and empowers us with the confidence to approach the Lord boldly. It purifies us so that the Holy Spirit can live and function in and through us. Repent and know that when we do, Jesus' blood covers the multitude of sins. Shame, guilt, and the legitimate charges against us from our life here on Earth are washed clean; we are made righteous through Jesus. God does not see what we see. No matter who judges us, stand on 1 Corinthians 4:3–4.

Prayer Starter: Lord, I am so thankful that because Jesus died for me and shed His blood, I am washed clean. I do not have to hold the guilt and shame for what I've done because the blood of Jesus washes me white as snow, and when You look at me, You see Jesus. You don't see me the way this world may judge me by or what I may even judge myself by. Help me, Lord, to see myself as You see me—a pure and holy vessel before You.

Day 74
The Bread: Spiritual Washing and Cleaning!
Acts 10:15; Matthew 23:26–28

The cleansing/cleaning inside our spiritual vehicle requires renewing our mind with the Word of God, prayer, fellowship, and working with the Holy Spirit who searches every bit of us behind doors we have closed, in hiding spots, under our behaviors and emotions, and it purifies us internally. The Holy Spirit is continually forming us into the internal image of Jesus Christ Himself. In Acts 10:15, God said to Peter, "Do not call anything unclean that God has cleaned"! In Matthew 23:26–28, Jesus said how they looked clean on the outside but were unclean on the inside. Jesus did not die for us so we would only have a washed vehicle. He died, so internally we would be clean—because we will become clean from the inside out regardless of the type of vehicle we drive. We have been created to exude the love, power, grace, mercy, all that God is, but this only truly happens when we allow the Holy Spirit to clean house, thus making our vehicle clean.

Thank goodness God is always willing to clean us up. He knows we get messy inside and out no matter what.

Prayer Starter: Lord, I can do everything I have to make sure that my outside looks clean; but my heart's desire is that I would emanate Your character, and I cannot do that, Lord, if I do not open the doors and allow You to clean me out thoroughly. Holy Spirit, I open the doors wide for You to work in me, cleaning out the crevices, the hiding spots, under my seats of shame, guilt, and feelings of worthlessness that I often sit in.

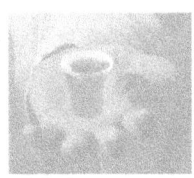

The Cup: The Flow from the Throne
Leviticus 19:2; Mark 1:10–11; Deuteronomy 31:8

*B*e holy because I, the Lord your God, am holy (Leviticus 19:2). We are holy because He is holy. The holiness of God flowed from His throne into and through His Son, Jesus, who sacrificed Himself for our redemption to God. When John baptized Jesus, God sent the Holy Spirit to dwell within Jesus, thus giving Him the full power and authority to do what God wanted of Him. That same Holy Spirit who was in Jesus, with Jesus, and carries the D.N.A. (Divine and Natural Authority) of God himself, now resides in us. You see, when Jesus ascended, He left the Holy Spirit here to live in us; thus, the D.N.A. (Divine and Natural Authority) of holiness is in us.

Drink of this cup in remembrance of the holiness you have that flows from the throne of God, through Jesus, and lives in you by the Holy Spirit.

The Lord himself goes before you and will be with you; He will never leave you nor forsake you (Deuteronomy 31:8).

Prayer Starter: Lord, thank you for Your Holy Spirit who lives in me, guiding me, and directing me—the same Holy Spirit who lived in Jesus, guiding and directing Him. Help me continually recognize the flow of Your love, Your power, Your anointing, everything You are that came to live in me through Your Holy Spirit.

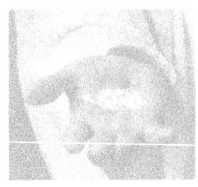
Day 75
The Bread & The Cup: Completion
Psalm 42:7

*O*n this last day of taking communion, spend some time thinking about this process we have just completed—75 days of communion. If we made it straight through, not missing a day, we can pat ourselves on the back, and we can know that we stuck to it and were able to have the persistence to push through daily. For those of us who may have missed a few days here and there because we forgot, life got in the way, or for whatever reason, we can know that Jesus is still patting us on the back because even in difficulty, challenge, burdens, whatever hindered us. Like Jesus was, we didn't give up when the enemy said, "Just quit! No one will know!" That is the time that God's Holy Spirit spoke louder in us to push on. Congratulations to all who accomplished these 75 days!

For this last day of taking the bread and the cup, STOP and look at the bread and the cup, and thank God for all you have experienced in this process. Thank Jesus for the sacrifices He made for you to be called the righteousness of the Lord. If you haven't already, share this devotion with your family, friends, groups, and church so they can be impacted as you have.

Prayer Starter: Lord, I thank you for all that I have learned throughout this amazing deep calling out to deep time in communion with You. I ask that You continue to speak to me and show me more of who You are and who I am in You. This experience has transformed me in so many ways, and I look forward to continuing to grow in You and with You, Lord.

YOUR GOD-GIVEN DIVINE & NATURAL AUTHORITY

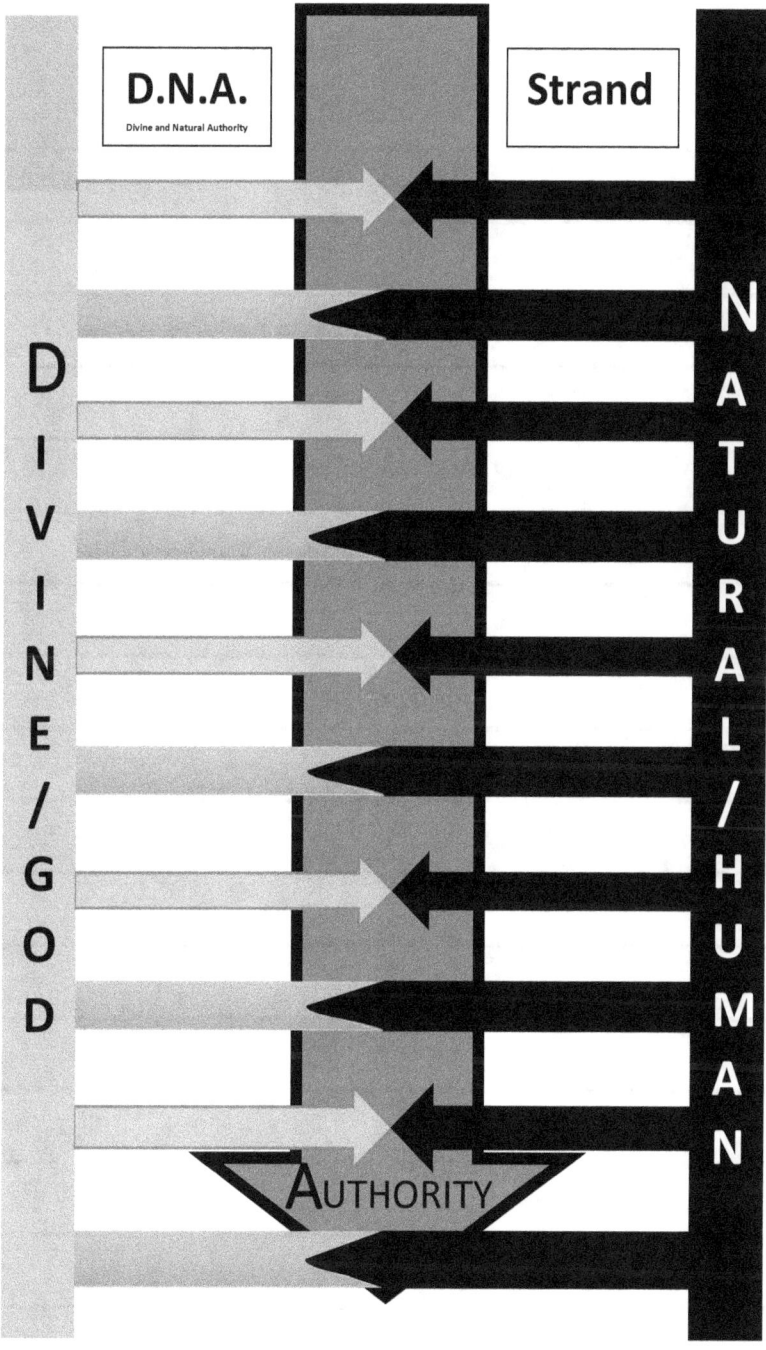

Notes

Acknowledgments

- My Lord God, Jesus my Savior, and the Holy Spirit that guides me and fills me with all of God, I am so grateful that I am redeemed, forgiven, and loved so much. How could I ever put enough words together to acknowledge my gratitude and love for You!
- Dave (Dad) and Leila (Mom) Anderson. I know I was not the easiest daughter. But you NEVER gave up on me! You took on the challenge of unconditional love, even when I made it difficult for you.
- Trina Gonzalez, thank you for your love and support, up close and at a distance, through the good, the bad, and the ugly. Forever sisters.
- The first 45 years of life experiences have helped educate, mold, and prepare me to be the woman God has now redeemed me to be today and has given me the earned authority for where God has purposed me to go.
- Prophet Shepherd Bushiri, Prophet Uebert Angel, Apostle Chris Oyakhilome, teachers who have provided me with mind-blowing revelatory knowledge and understanding. They are mighty men of God who have inspired me to dig deeper in the Word and have transformed my understanding of God, the Word, and who I am in God.
- Spokane Faith Center, where I learned and grew in God. All who stood by me through many good and difficult times while I lived in Spokane, Washington.
- Pastor LaShund and Kadesha Lambert, I thank you for your friendship. I appreciate that you both have always been so supportive of me.
- Destiny Ministry Training Center in Spokane, where I received my AA in Ministerial Studies.

- "The Bible Lady," for the impactful Bible Studies and your friendship during and following a very life-changing time.
- Shara Cooper, thank you for being there during my lowest point and speaking hope and life into me that transformed my understanding of God's grace and mercy. I will never forget you and pray unceasingly for your release.
- Cathedral of Pentecost, where I have been welcomed, embraced, and allowed to grow in this next step of God's plan for me.
- Russell Womack, my first-ever editor, who has been so supportive of this book and impacted by it as he read and edited. You have inspired me to push forward and truly realize how important it is for this book to be published.

About the Author

Although she encountered God in her youth, S. Sylvi Anderson was not supernaturally transformed until 2017.

For decades, she lived the duality of outstanding achievements, including an AA in Ministry Studies and a Master's in Occupational Therapy with a highly successful career and financial security while simultaneously walking a path of self-destruction.

At rock bottom, she finally found salvation and redemption in Jesus. Since 2017, God has fast-tracked her re-education process in who He is. Her life experiences have given her earned authority in understanding the power of God's redemption and recognition of His purpose for humankind.

During this season of life, S. Sylvi makes her home in South Florida.

www.ingramcontent.com/pod-product-compliance
Lightning Source LLC
LaVergne TN
LVHW021701060526
838200LV00050B/2462